16 95

A Passion for ACTING

Exploring the Creative Process

A Passion for
ACTING
Exploring the Creative Process

ALLAN MILLER

BACK STAGE BOOKS

An imprint of Watson-Guptill Publications /New York

Edited by Fred Weiler
Cover and book design by Jay Anning

Photo/illustration credits: Stephanie Maze (p. 114), Harrison Houlé (pp. 113, 115),
Manuel de Muga's GAUDI, published by Rizzoli, New York (p.116).

Library of Congress Cataloging-in-Publication Data
Miller, Allan.
    A passion for acting: exploring the creative process/
by Allan Miller.
       p. cm.
     ISBN 0-8230-8254-7
     1. Acting. I. Title.
PN2061.M45 1992
792'.028—dc20
    91-44332
                             CIP

Manufactured in the United States of America

First printing, 1992

1 2 3 4 5 6 7 8 / 99 98 97 96 95 94 93 92

For Laura Zucker,
who inspired this book,
then made me write it

Notes and Acknowledgments

Throughout the book, I have decided to use the designation "actor" whether it refers to a man or a woman. In addition, to simplify matters, I am using "he" to refer to both male and female persons.

You will notice more incidents in this book that took place at the Actors Studio than in any other locale. This does not mean that I believe the Studio/Strasberg approach is inherently more important than others. The simple reason is that I was there longer than anywhere else, and that because of its worldwide influence, the Actors Studio happened to attract as guests some of the most outstanding actors of my time.

There also happen to be more stories in the book involving Barbra Streisand than any other single actor. Because she was just fifteen when I first began working with her, her naiveté (about acting as well as many other matters in life), her hunger for knowledge, and her willingness to try anything she could follow, gave me challenges and opportunities to use everything I thought I knew about actor training. And when those techniques didn't work, I was forced to devise others that did.

I want to thank the people who gave me invaluable help in shaping the first draft of this book through their good notes: Gregory Miller, Beth Lapides, Dr. Lewis Miller, Martin E. Brooks, Jenny O'Hara, Nick Ullet, John Schuck, and Harrison Houlé.

Contents

Appetite

Despite monumental ignorance of actors' processes of work, tens of thousands of young (and sometimes older) people join the acting ranks every year. For some, it's the glint of fame and glamour that catches their desires. For most aspiring actors—from my experience—there is the larger need for validation of self, the acknowledgment that the thoughts and feelings of an individual have the right to be expressed.

And talent be damned. I remember way back in grammar school a singing teacher lining us all up, making us imitate her la-la-la-la scale one at a time. Then she separated us on the spot into singers and non-singers. For years I didn't believe I could sing because of that teacher.

Talent is an aptitude for expression in a given medium. Some of us have less aptitude than others. So what? It doesn't mean we don't have any.

Give me people with enough *appetite*, and within a reasonable amount of time, I can train them to act well. We all have deep, secret feelings. With enough craft and discipline, they can be connected to our work. Even if we don't achieve greatness, even if we sometimes fail, if we stay connected to our deepest feelings and attitudes towards life, we will find gratification and a sense of accomplishment.

This applies to all walks of life, to all cultures. No matter where we work, or how, the need to feel expressive is universal.

I have taught semiliterate teenagers in Harlem, Irish actors in Dublin, a class of lawyers-to-be at New York University, a gathering of corporate heads in Canada, university students on the east and west coasts, graduate students at the Yale School of Drama, aspiring actors from all over the country, and actors already cast in plays, films, and television. I've even taught a casting agent. The one requisite measure of any of their talents was appetite, the degree to which they hungered to express themselves. All else followed.

The path to creative imagination—and even inspiration—is lined with good, sensible, structured stepping stones of craft. We can all walk that path with training. Every human being has infinitely more capacity to live imaginatively than our usual habits permit. It is craft that allows our imaginations to flourish.

That's what this book is about.

Inspiration

My first awareness of a certain presumption in my acting work came when I had my first paid job in television. I was an Indian on a live telecast of an adaptation of James Fenimore Cooper's novel *The Deerslayer*. (Those were the days when you could walk into an agent's office completely unknown, and be cast in a role that only required you to be six feet tall and dark-haired.) There were at least twenty of us actor-Indians on the show, all tall and all dark. None of us had any lines, but we all wore wigs; some of us added war paint and feathers in the make-up room. Because I thought acting was the opposite of being in the army, I volunteered for all the extra action I could get to fatten my part. The director liked my enthusiasm well enough to choose me to be the single Indian who came close to scalping the Deerslayer himself. Tomahawk in hand, I pursued him relentlessly until a shot killed me. At the end of the show, fiercely proud of the special business I'd been given to do, I called home. My mother, of course, had watched, along with half the neighborhood.

"How did you like it?" I asked.

"Very good," she said. "It was wonderful."

"You really liked it?" I said.

"Of course, it was very good."

"What about me?"

"Wonderful," she said. "You were very good." A pause, then before I could think of something else to say, she continued: "But which Indian were you?"

The reverberations of that question have bent and shaped the rest of my professional life.

Was I so indistinguishable from my fellow actor-Indians? Were there no special physical or vocal attributes I possessed to single me out from the mass? No character qualities, no emotional displays to clue even my mother in to my actor-creative being?

Not really. Using make-up, a wig, and an Indian outfit, I had hidden my urban self fairly successfully—but at the same time, no

1

unique character had emerged. I had the desire to be an unusually good actor, but none of the tools.

I certainly didn't want to be thought of as conventional, predictable, or banal as an actor. But what did inventiveness or imagination mean when doing a role? How would I ever get to be like that? How in the world did anyone become inspired in acting? How could I even define inspiration, since by its very nature it can't be known until it occurs?

Sometime soon after the Indian event, my mother was instrumental in making me face another artistic issue. One Sunday evening, feeling the communication gap (or guilt) of not having spoken to my parents in weeks, I called. My mother answered. During our conversation, I inquired about the subject of that week's moviegoing (my parents saw one film a week, religiously).

"It wasn't very good," said my mother.

"Really?" I asked. (Seeing that one film a week was usually a treat.) "What was it?"

"Ohh, *The Conqueror*," came the reply.

"*The Conqueror?*"

"Yeah, with John Wayne."

"I don't understand, Mom. You love John Wayne."

"Yeah," she said, "but this time, I don't know, he didn't fit the part."

John Wayne didn't fit a part? This I had to see. I went to a nearby movie theater and sure enough, there was the big guy, up on a horse, hardly talking. But when he did talk, it just didn't sound like Genghis Khan, and that's who he was playing. Even my untutored film-critic-mother knew the difference. And John Wayne never did another costume drama. He just didn't fit those parts.

As an actor, I wanted to fit lots of parts. And I wanted to be creative and imaginative like Alfred Lunt or Spencer Tracy or Laurence Olivier or Paul Muni—actors whose ranges were wide and formidable, who seemed limitless in their characterizations, but who also seemed able to maintain a persona of their own. And they were all stage-trained. They'd all been discovered on stage to begin their film careers. So the stage is where my focus went. I began searching out acting teachers who were known for training the better stage actors.

One of my earliest was Uta Hagen. She was wonderful: strong but understanding, with a real grasp of the skills necessary for the higher levels of professional acting. Her methods and criticisms brought all the students in my class, regardless of any prior training, to finer levels of acting work. All of us became increasingly and steadily effective in our scenes, and in our outside auditions. All of us, except one. That one was Geraldine Page. She was beyond good; she was marvelous. She was fascinating, provocative, mischievous—everything. Her range of emotions seemed infinite, her character work surprising and insightful, her own persona shy and warm. I wanted my acting to be more like hers, but I didn't know how.

At the end of almost every scene Geraldine did in that class, a strange pattern occurred. The rest of us, at the end of our scenes, would try to report as clearly as we could the overall "objective," and then the "beats" of our respective scenes. (That's how Uta taught in those days: first, define and choose a single through-line of action for the character, and then the pieces, the beats, that it was composed of.) But Gerry invariably suffered the trials of the damned trying to express what she had done.

"Oh Uta," Geraldine would slightly wail. "I don't know exactly what I did. I think I tried to...uhm...ohh...I'm not sure. I don't think I really did my objective. I think maybe..." And Uta would jump in to rescue her. With great regard and careful guidance, she would state some action Geraldine had taken, or a reading of a line, and then say something like, "When you did that, weren't you really trying to accomplish that objective?" or, "When you said that line, wasn't that the beginning of one of your beats?"

Geraldine would usually have her head half-lowered by then, sometimes with tears in her eyes. She would try desperately to grasp the meaning of what Uta was so staunchly asserting. In the absence of a clear affirmative from Geraldine, Uta would whip around to face the class and make us the judge: "When Gerry was doing so and so, wasn't she really trying to do such and such?"

And of course we were all thrilled to be able to say, "Yes she was. Sure she was."

I had always accepted the pattern. But I had also always known that when Geraldine acted, she did something else besides her objectives and beats that no one—including Gerry—ever acknowledged. We all ascribed these other things she did to her talent, which we were willing to admit seemed beyond ours.

A few years later, after I had become a member of the Actors Studio, I did one of my more successful scenes there by trying an experiment. From watching the ways our teacher Lee Strasberg tried to elicit more imaginative work from those in the class, I decided to test one of his ideas by choosing a scene from the play *Climate of Eden* (which I had seen rather poorly performed by the actor in the lead role on Broadway). My role was a man in his thirties, with a somewhat dark and repressive past, who takes advantage of an invitation to visit a jungle-living family. He wants to sort out his life and heal some of the terrible wounds of his past.

I made an actual list, like a laundry list, of what was physically true for the character, and concentrated only on those items for the scene. There were a total of eleven physical elements. I learned the lines, of course, but in the few rehearsals I had with my partner, who was wonderfully open to my exploration, I did anything that occurred to me about each of my numbered physical truths as I went down my list. I didn't always stay in numerical order. One item on my list was that he was a writer, so wherever I went I carried a pen and pad with me, and practiced writing down conversations or phrases or descriptions of interesting things or actions I came in contact with. I continued to do the same during our scene presentation.

Another item on the list was that the character kept his wife's will near or on him at all times. I wrote out an imaginary will that combined elements of my own wife's life as well as the character's, and every once in a while, I would take it out of my jacket and re-read it. I did this during the scene, too.

The play specified that he was recovering from a mental breakdown. I gave myself the imagined choice that because of a tumor, part of my brain had been operated on and left void. And I tried to behave as if that were true.

I won't bother to detail the eight other items on my list. Suffice it to say that they all kept me very busy and involved as we went through the scene. I'd never been easier with myself working at the Studio. I felt focused and exploratory.

When it was over—it took approximately twenty minutes—Strasberg was smiling. His usual comment at the end of a scene or an exercise was "All right, what do you want to tell us?" This time he turned to the class and said, "Wait a minute. Before we hear from Allan, I want to know how many people think he was working on one thing with a lot of elements in it, or a lot of *different things?*"

When he threw down a gauntlet like that, most of the actors in the room tended to fall silent. That's what happened this time. In the silence, without waiting very long, Strasberg wheeled around and called to me, "I thought it was one task with a lot of things in it."

I beamed—it was always such a treat to be able to contradict him. "No," I yelled out. "It was all different things. Eleven, to be exact!"

He laughed, very curious, and asked me to describe them. I took out my list, still kept in my pocket for reference, and began to read them out by number. He nodded in recognition several times. Then when I finished and explained what my list was for, he suddenly said, "What was the shivering you did when you were standing by the window? I didn't hear that on your list."

"Shivering?" I asked. Then, before he could repeat himself, I realized the moment he was talking about. "Oh, that really wasn't on the list. It's just what happened to me as I was shifting my attention from number three to number four." Everyone laughed but Strasberg. Pleased as he was with what I had done, he was serious as he leaned forward and said, "Do more of what happened between the numbers. It's important for you."

Suddenly, this day at the Actors Studio, in the middle of Lee Strasberg's comments on my laundry-list approach to scene work, I realized that his remark about doing more *between* my numbers was what had made Geraldine Page's acting so wondrous in that earlier acting class. She allowed whatever happened *to her*, as she tried to fulfill her choices for her character, to become visible, to become part and parcel of her scenes. That's what kept her so spontaneous and surprising, so fluid and affecting. That, and her other choices, of course.

Soon after this event at the Studio, I read of an exciting production of *King Lear*, directed by Peter Brook. This new British *wunderkind* had already become known worldwide for his avant-garde, ensemble approach to Shakespeare as well as contemporary plays. His production of *Lear* starred Paul Scofield, one of England's greater actors.

I tried to find out everything I could about how Brook worked on the play, and eventually discovered quite a lot. There were two particular events that intrigued me, both of which happened toward the end of the rehearsal period.

The first one concerned difficulties in working out interpretations for several of the major characters in the play. One of Brook's continuing dilemmas was how to arrive at less calculated behavior for Scofield's Lear.

Mr. Scofield was a traditionally-trained British actor: logic, coherence, great vocal prowess, and restrained emotionalism were essential components of his acting style. Improvisations, or surprises of any sort, were not.

During rehearsals, when Lear is asked by his eldest daughter to leave her house, Brook was dissatisfied with Scofield's responses. At one of the final run-throughs, having a full set to work with, Scofield's reaction to his daughter's expulsion was still not quite right. Brook called to the actor from the audience, "Paul, *do* something to express your displeasure."

Given that sudden permission, Scofield grabbed one of the long tables onstage and flipped it and its contents onto the floor. Delighted with this action, Brook called out, "You retainers, do more of what your master has done." Instantly, the actors playing Lear's soldiers laid hold of every movable piece of furniture and let it fly.

It was a devastating demonstration, which pleased Brook to no end (but which, of course, nearly gave the set designer a heart attack). And though no one was hurt, and all involved felt excited by what they had done, the actors were never able to recapture the spontaneity of that sequence.

The second event that intrigued me occurred at one of the last dress rehearsals. So much tension and anxiety had built up within the company that Scofield had asked for a no-audience performance. Other than Brook and members of the staff, the only person to be allowed in the theater would be the designated still photographer with his camera and tripod.

As the performance progressed, there seemed to be no rise of excitement from the company, no special moments, no changes in tone or delivery to separate this night from the rest of the week's work; the only difference was the presence of the photographer and his ever-whirring camera. Suddenly, with no warning whatsoever, Scofield turned around to face the auditorium, unhooked his cape, flung it in the direction of the photographer, and hissed "Get that man out of here," then returned to the action onstage. Brook's assistant noted in his diary, "It was an electric moment we wished we could have kept in the production."

Here they were, two more examples of an actor's *own* response to a situation in the play becoming more expressive than the character's. Geraldine knew how to fuse hers with the character's; in the case of *Lear*, Scofield and Brook didn't.

Thinking about this business of spontaneity and inspiration, I began to question not only my acting approaches but my responses in life as well. So many of them seemed pre-chosen: the kinds of greetings I always gave my postman or grocery clerk, the attitudes I almost always used when calling my parents (or when they called me), the niceties (and not-so-niceties) of my behavior with friends. Everything felt so habitual, so ordered. How was it possible to be spontaneous when I was always so prepared to do only what was expected of me?

I knew that inspiration couldn't be summoned on command, yet it didn't seem accidental when I saw it in other people's work. How could I reach such a state? How could anyone?

Most of us are taught at an early age by parents, teachers, and others to know what we are doing, to be responsible for our actions, to be adult and mature as we grow out of childhood. But in infancy, we are allowed and encouraged to be completely open to everything—sounds, tastes, smells, faces, objects, everything—and we grow. We gain daily in confidence and daring for weeks, months, and (hopefully) years. We learn through a combination of responses, instruction, and *the freedom to try things out.* As long as we don't have to come up with the right answers, anything can occur. Once we know how things *should* be, questions and curiosity fade.

Albert Einstein was often asked how he had ever conceived of his awesome theories. His reply was always the same: "I had to ask myself, why *do* those tiny lights twinkle in the heavens? Just like children ask. Then I began to wonder."

In his fifties, Picasso and his friend Matisse were guests at an exhibition of children's drawings when Picasso said, "You know, Henri, by the time I was fifteen, I could paint as well as Raphael. All the rest of my life, I've been learning to paint like these children."

Like children.

We've all seen hundreds of children's paintings and drawings over the years at airports, in banks, and in schools. Their subjects are always the same: trees, cars, buildings, flowers, airplanes, parents, children, animals. If we were able to gather all the children's drawings from all over the world, ever since children began to draw, how many would there be now? Billions? Trillions? And wouldn't all their subject matter tend to be the same, differentiated only by culture or circumstance? Rather predictable, conventional, and banal.

But would anyone ever accuse a child of being these? How could we, when every single drawing is original? Original and imaginative—and sometimes, yes, inspired. No two children ever draw the same subject in exactly the same way. The drawings or paintings are all unique. And they will continue to be unique, because no criteria for drawing has yet been established for these young children to follow. They are unaware of standards. Children are free to try out any mixture of colors or paper or crayons for any of their subject matters in any form they choose. They are free to be inventive.

Until a certain age. Then along come their well-meaning parents and teachers—who up to now have been so encouraging and allowing—suggesting that the animal in the drawing could look even more like a dog or cat if they would learn how to draw *better* so everyone could know *for sure* that it was a dog or cat.

So originality and individuality begin to fade. They are no longer nurtured; other values interfere.

By the time most children have become adults, their means and manners of expression have been diluted, deflected, and suppressed. As adults, we try too hard to live up to previously-established limits of acceptability for expression. And that is why so few of us ever feel imaginative and inventive or inspired in our lives and in our acting. We have given up availability for acceptance, curiosity for presumption. We need to remind ourselves that for inspiration to occur, our minds must be like children's: guileless and available.

The door to individuality and inspiration is to be found in a state of childlike openness. The hinge that always keeps that door open for actors is *allowing your own thoughts, feelings and sensations to become expressible while you are acting the choices you, or you and the director, have made for the part.* You must not presume that you have less to offer than others; you have differences to offer. You must keep those differences alive and included.

Unfortunately, it has been my experience that more people than not actually believe that acting well is really a form of magic—some sort of mantle descends from heaven at prescribed times to guide a chosen actor into the realms of inspiration. No one seems to know when it will happen, or why, but somehow a small select group of actors is regularly selected to benefit from its effects.

Acting, at its highest levels, is *not* the result of any deity-inspired supernatural power. Quite the contrary, it comes from a merging of the individual actor's persona with characteristics of the role he or she is playing.

There are principles of human behavior that arouse the best of actors into their most creative states. It is these principles that I hope the next chapters will help you understand and explore.

Relaxation

In the late 1940s, there was a popular song called "Let Yourself Go," whose lyrics spoke for a multitude of people's needs and desires:

> Let yourself go, relax
> Let yourself go, relax
> You've got yourself tied up in a knot
> The night is cold but the music's hot...
> So let yourself go.

Sounds wonderful, even now. If you've gotten yourself "tied up in a knot" because of whatever circumstances, including feeling all alone on a cold night, get out there with some "hot" music and dance. Get it all out.

We all face these "knots" regularly. And we all suffer the same consequences if we don't or can't remove the circumstances that cause our dilemmas: we become tense, wary, defensive, and ultimately worn down. Our systems rebel, the exquisite machinery of our bodies break down, and we suffer mightily, from migraines to heart attacks.

Some of the best-selling over-the-counter medicines and drugs in this country are those that offer relief from headaches and upset stomachs. Both of these problems are mostly precipitated by tensions, by feelings we don't express, and/or by overworking our muscular and nervous systems.

It's fascinating to watch athletes at the Olympics gather just before an event. These incredibly well-trained young women and men gulp air, gyrate their arms and legs, trot up and down, kneel and kick, even roll over on their backs in a sudden, mad effort to remove last-minute kinks and tensions that may hold them back. They have labored ceaselessly for four years just to be ready for this one-day, one-time activity. What's wrong with these athletes? How come they're so tense after all that training?

11

We all know why: hopes, expectations, and dreams are also on the line that Olympic day. Sacrifices, parental and peer concerns, the specter of failure haunts these athletes.

The same hopes and concerns surround each of us in our own chosen fields of endeavor. And in our personal relationships.

A friend indeed is someone we can call on at a moment's notice to listen to our woes, our frustrations, and our needs, and who is capable of steadying us with words like, "It's okay. You're going to be all right. Relax a little. Take it easy. Tell me all about it."

We need that: reassurance, someone to tell us we're allowed to get it all out. But how? Some friends will suggest a long walk to distract us, others will suggest a cup of coffee or a drink to warm our insides, some will suggest a few days away to help settle our minds and feelings and gain some perspective. No one has yet found a single formula that will assuage all the anxieties we face in life.

Rex Harrison was, for generations of audiences, the personification of the witty, urbane, and outwardly relaxed Englishman on stage and in films. Yet late in his life he complained to the *New York Times* that it was "so annoying to find oneself referred to as the 'unflappable' Rex Harrison. Unflappable, my arse! I can play the part as well as the next one, but don't mistake performance for reality. No one—I say again—no one with an ounce of talent was ever *truly* relaxed before an audience."

The word "relax" itself has been badly misused in our vocabulary. In social situations, whenever I've heard one person suggest that another person relax, the implication was to get more comfortable, more settled.

That's a dictionary kind of meaning, and a perfectly serviceable one. If you look up the word "relax," its definitions will include: to reduce concentration or application, to lessen effort, to seek recreation.

But suppose the task is to relax *into* one's work? A piano mover or weightlifter must exert muscular effort to do the job. A riveter has to apply terrific physical pressure to the rivet gun or it will pull out of his hands. A lumberjack has to hunch his shoulder, back, and arm muscles to hold a power saw to a large tree. Muscular tension is an integral part of these types of work.

But what if each of these workers was able to limit the areas of tension so that the tension never interfered with the performance of the job? Like a good surgeon, who despite enormous anxieties and long hours at the operating table, is capable of keeping his fingers supple and dexterous. The surgeon has learned that while he is on a life-saving job, nothing must interfere with the workings of his hands.

The same is true of any good piano mover, weightlifter, riveter, and lumberjack. The good ones learn to use only the amount of physical energy necessary to the performance of their work. Therefore, they are as relaxed as possible in their work.

So one of my definitions of relaxation—one you will not find in the dictionary—is "using the least amount of energy necessary to accomplish a given task." Lifting a chair shouldn't require the same amount of muscular energy as moving a piano. Writing a letter should not necessitate hunching your back and shoulders like a lumberjack. Plucking a rose should never involve nearly the strain of weightlifting.

Even more important for actors is finding a process of relaxing into one's work that allows *any and all responses to occur* while one is working. Like a baby, who is sometimes the most intense of us all. Babies cry when they are hurt or unhappy (they don't worry about being called a cry-baby). Babies can smile and drool at the same time their toes curl and they fart (they don't worry about looking stupid or foolish). And if we don't interfere with their responses, but support them and minister to their needs, they stay bubbling and happy, involved and inquisitive. They don't tense up, because no one has yet told them their responses are inappropriate.

As actors or people, we must understand that to explore our innermost feelings and visions of life—to get into them and to learn about our capacities to respond—we must be open to what we find without prejudgment. We must relax *into* our reactions, whatever they may be.

Have you ever had the experience of being out in fierce cold weather, finally making your way into a warm room—and only then beginning to shiver? While you were outside, your body tensed up against the cold. When you reached the warm room you "relaxed," letting down your guard, and your body was finally able to express the cold it felt by shivering. For those first few moments indoors, you may actually have felt colder than when you were outside.

In a dentist's chair, we aren't able to "relax" as the drill begins to bite into our teeth because we presume it's going to hurt. Even with an injection of Novocain, as the first moment of the drill's contact approaches, we flinch involuntarily to avoid the possibility of pain. It takes a good while before we realize that because of the injection there is no pain, and we can relax.

The same is true with too many of our reactions. We've all been trained to monitor our feelings, to try to pick out which are permissible depending on the situation, and which are not. Up to a certain age, crying and yelling if the dentist hurts us is tolerated; an adult is expected to take it. As a child, jumping up and down with excitement in a candy shop is allowable, but just try it as an adult. Instead of expressing our immediate and full response to the pain in the dentist's office or the goodies in the shop, we push the feelings away, consider them wrong, and finally modulate them to a more socially acceptable level of response. We unconsciously begin to tense our muscles to hold down these unwanted responses. And after many years of conditioning, we build an army of muscular defenses to remove or neutralize "excessive" reactions in social and private situations.

To play a multitude of characters, actors must reverse the process of muscular defense. They must have immediately available the entire panoply of feelings that a human being is capable of, or every role will be bent to whatever narrow range of responses the actors themselves have been limited to.

To be at their best when rehearsing or exercising, actors must permit all feelings and impulses to arise, and only later should they begin to define those they find most appropriate to the roles they're working on.

Do you know how a lie detector works? Even if you don't, I'm sure you have some idea of the kinds of measuring devices doctors and hospitals use to monitor heart rate or blood pressure. Whether it's a device to test our ability to tell the truth, or a machine that mirrors the truths of our bodily functions, the principle underlying the use of these instruments is the same. All human feelings are in reality neurological: chemical or electrical charges triggered in the brain by stimuli coming in through our senses. These charges, which we then translate in our minds into experiences of love or pain or pleasure or anxiety, can all be measured objectively.

Which means that what we all relate to as our feelings from the multitudinous experiences of life register first as chemical or electrical impulses inside our bodies—impulses about which we often have no conscious knowledge. They exist only within the parameters of our nervous system, which picks up these impulses and sends them on to our brain cells for translation. Sometimes they occur so quickly, or in such a mixture of signals, we are unable to decipher them. So we let them pass or we ignore them. But even when our brains reject these little shocks of sensation and feeling, they will continue to register in our bodies.

The true search for our feelings, therefore, has to start with our bodies. Whatever labels we want to put on these neurological jolts within ourselves—"happiness," "anguish," "ecstasy"—can come later. Or not at all. What is necessary is to acknowledge any degree of sensation in our arms, our legs, our feet, our backs, our necks, and yes, our heads. Our bodies contain thousands of nerves. They usually function in groupings large enough to register messages we can convey to other people. We all know when we have a toothache. We all know what we mean by a feeling of relief. But until there is a medical or therapeutic necessity to observe and mark down the smallest details of our bodily responses, we blithely generalize what we are feeling.

Actors must become more sensitive to the experiences of life than most mortals because they are expected to register the full range of the human condition for the rest of mankind. Their instruments are their entire selves. The part of the actor's self that most registers this sensitivity is his body.

So as a process of physical relaxation is applied, it must also include simultaneous recognition of whatever small or large charges may be aroused in our bodily housings. And these little shocks or nerve impulses *must be given vocal outlet.* Noises and sounds must accompany any relaxation procedure to reach the full range of our responsive capacities. Our own everyday expressions are too limiting. By the time we find proper emotionally-toned words to describe a sensation, the feeling itself may have dissipated or mutated into something else.

All genuine emotion is mixed. No one is ever just happy, except in cartoons. You may feel expansive and lightheaded, which makes you describe your condition as happy. But that happiness has various components: it may make you feel available, more considerate—even concerned that you are unable to make someone else feel as happy as you are. Emotion shifts and slides, becomes other than itself, more than itself. The surest path to keeping up with these changes and gradations of feeling is through the use of sounds. We must relearn the sounds of every experience and sensation to which we respond. Only then, when we speak as actors in a role, will we encompass everything our characters can be thinking and feeling. The wider our range of expression, the wider our creative lives.

Stop right now and try it. The book can wait. Check yourself over and try to feel what's going on with you and your body. Any pressures anywhere? Sound them out. Any tightness in the eyes or mouth, or where one leg is crossed over the other? Articulate these tightnesses. On a scale of one to ten, which ones are a three? Which ones are an eight? Any numbness from sitting too long? How would you put that into noises? Not complaints, just try to be objective about it—like Dr. Jekyll making notes on his transition into Mr. Hyde (only your notes will be verbal). Look for good sensations. Are you feeling supple in your neck or arms, is your digestive system warmly peaceful? Wouldn't hurt to put these sensations into sound, too.

Now you need some kind of structure—let's call it a ritual—for this whole process. Religions of all persuasions have always recognized that to induce a spiritual receptivity, a physical ritual is first necessary. A penitent in the Catholic church begins the process of salvation by kneeling and crossing herself; Hindu gurus insist on a yoga cross-legged position, hands palm up, while maintaining a chant, in order to enter such a state.

Even in ordinary, everyday business, a handshake (or a mutual bow in Japan) is required to suggest an openness of mind and spirit to the coming discussion.

The world's cultures have demonstrated infinite ingenuity in creating these rituals and they have endured over centuries, but almost none of us has been conditioned to a personal ritual for self-expression.

Here is mine. It is a physical ritual to achieve relaxation, and thereby to enter the realm of true expression.

Take a seat on any piece of furniture that has a firm back. Think of this chair or perch as a seat for a long trip on a plane, train, bus, or car. You know you'd have to maintain yourself in a relatively cramped space without your leg or arm falling asleep. And you know you wouldn't want to end up with a stiff neck. So you would make minor adjustments to different parts of your body as time wore on. Do the same as you continue sitting in your chair. Feel free at any time to make adjustments necessary to keep your blood flowing and your body in a reasonably supple state. Give yourself a minute or two to set-tle into a sustainable position and then check your breathing.

Most of us really don't breathe well, you know? In many of our everyday activities, especially relationship situations, we all tend to be rather shallow-breathed. Sure, once in a while we breathe deeply, and frequently sigh, but then we go right back to the half-breathing we are used to. We need blood in our bodies to live and function. All nutrients are carried by our bloodstream. The more open the flow of this red river, the fuller and longer lives we can lead. When one of our limbs "falls asleep," it is really going numb from a lack of blood. The same is true for our brains: cut off enough blood supply to our minds, and they go numb. We cut off our blood supply by tensing ourselves, or even by crossing our legs while sitting in an office or at a party. Pinch or squeeze your muscles anywhere in your body and you will lessen the nat-ural course of blood in that area. Relax those muscles and you immediately enrich that same area. But you cannot relax your muscles while you're busy restricting your breathing.

So breathe. Deeply. With your mouth slightly open. And from the abdomen, not from the chest. (When you are deeply asleep, the natu-ral, normal relaxed breathing that you do can be seen by the rise and

fall of your stomach, not your chest.) And as you breathe, sigh, some-
times soundlessly, sometimes adding the sounds of the energies being
released.

Another way of thinking about these sounds and noises I keep
urging you to make is to imagine yourself in a foreign country
where no one speaks anything close to your language. You have
a serious pain in your body and need a doctor. How would you
convey to him what your body is going through? Only through a
series of illustrated movements and noises that would express a
condition such as a circular throbbing pressure in your stomach, a
sizzling shooting pain in your back, or a wave of shivers across
your chest and arms. Or try to imagine yourself in that same foreign country after a sumptuous, delicious meal, trying to express
to your hosts the measure of your gratitude, and the different
pleasures of the foods that were served. You could easily spend
several minutes trying to describe how you progressed from the
appetizers to dessert. It's the effect on your body that you are trying to vocalize.

I recommend starting the next part of this procedure at the
head because this area tends to be where the most *involuntary*
muscle activity takes place. You know how your eyes blink to
avoid a dust particle in the air before your brain even registers the
action? Most people's tics, and anyone's stutter, are activated in
the facial muscles. We sometimes tense these muscles all day long
to prevent ourselves and others from seeing how we really feel.
These are the muscles that need the most continual relaxation.

Now think of your body as constructed in circling horizontal bands,
each band approximately four inches in height. Start at the very top of
your head, so that the first band ends at the bridge of your nose. Try to
locate all the muscles in this band by flexing them. (You know how
some people are able to move their scalps back and forth? There are
muscles up there. You may not have consciously moved them in your
entire life, but they're there. So look for them.) Flex the muscles and
hold them, then release them. Repeat that. Flex them and hold them,
then release them. With your mind's eye, imagine those muscles even
deeper under the skin than you can first feel, and try to flex, hold, and

release them as deeply as you can. Continue to breathe well. Don't push the breathing as you would in a doctor's office; make it as effortless as possible. It's the placement, not the intensity, you're looking for. And encourage yourself to make noises as you flex, hold, and release.

Without ignoring the first band, move down to the next, which will run roughly from the top of your nose to your upper lip. You'll find lots of small muscles readily available in this band, but search thoroughly for them. Circle your head, make sure you find the muscles that control your ears. (There are a good number of people who've learned to wiggle them.) See if you can move any part of the back of your head. Get in under the skin. And, while you are checking into these areas, remind yourself of that first band, and lightly re-flex some of the muscles you found there.

Stay aware of your breathing. Keep it alive, keep it coming from your gut. Check your stomach muscles to make sure they're pumping your breath out, not just in. Make sounds.

And move on to the next band. It's not necessary to resolve every suggestion of tension in any band before moving onto the next. Set yourself the goal of no longer than six or seven minutes to reach the lowest band of your body. Within a few weeks, you should easily be able to do it in less than three minutes. It's a process of relaxation you must learn to continue in rehearsals and then on into performance. It will become your singular necessity for entering a creative state.

Remember, you are adding *bands as you descend your body, one connected to the other. Never discard or ignore any. And never leave off making sounds commensurate with the energies released or stirred within you. If loud sounds are impossible (perhaps a loved one nearby is trying to sleep), make them silently. Mouth them as in a dumb show. But always do them to the degree that you experience the energy in your body.*

By the fourth band, you have entered the upper arms, shoulders, and chest. You now have the choice of concentrating on your arms alone, and moving down them until you reach your hands, then moving your focus back to your upper chest and on down the torso, or you can think of your shoulders, arms, and chest as one physical entity. Try either way. Or alternate approaches from time to time, as a minor form of refreshment. And continue relaxing these bands all the way down your body to your feet.

Don't obligate yourself to unknotting every area of tension you come upon; it's enough in this first stage that your inner eye becomes accustomed to searching out these resistant pockets. On any given day, you will find the specific tensions of the day before may have shifted. One day's practice will require more time spent with your neck; the following day, the most difficult area will be your ankles or calves. When you practice this exercise immediately after waking up, you may be surprised to find more muscular knots than later that same day. We are complex creatures, and very clever with our inner prohibitions: we sometimes become more tense during sleep than when we're awake. Trust that eventually this all-encompassing physical and vocal exercise will gain you real insight into, and control of, the enormous energies and feelings that we all possess.

The following is a concrete example of what this process, almost all by itself, can accomplish in actual performance.

In my earlier years of teaching, one of my youngest students was Barbra Streisand (before she took the "a" out of Barbara). Within a short time, her singing career was skyrocketing, but even with a burgeoning schedule of television and stage work, she would return to perform on weekends at a small nightclub in Greenwich Village called the Bon Soir.

On one of these return visits, as she had done regularly in the past, she called me to come see how she was doing. It was a Friday night, and the place was packed. I went right to my table, and soon she was onstage doing her first number.

It was a little muted, as was the rest of the set. Her voice was thrilling, but she seemed distant—sort of cautious—which was unusual for Barbra when she sang.

In her dressing room, she apologized. "I forgot you were coming tonight. Don't say anything, okay? I was just too tired. I was doing a TV show all day. I should've canceled tonight."

"Do you have to do the second set?" I asked.

"What do you mean? All those people out there, what am I going to do with them?"

"Well," I said, "when you're tired, you have to sing tired."

"Yeah, sure," she chuckled.

And that was all there was to that. We exchanged a few personal remarks. Someone brought her in a snack, I excused myself, and she invited me back the following week.

I went to the bar, where I was less visible from the stage, ordered a drink, and waited. Her trio played a couple of introductory numbers (they were terrific musicians) and the lights dimmed as they segued into Barbra's opening number, a jump tune called "Keeping Out Of Mischief Now."

It wasn't sung much differently than in the first set. She clearly didn't know I had stayed, so in the darkness, I quietly made my way toward the exit, thinking, Hey, you win some, you lose some. But all of a sudden, behind me I heard her saying, "Wait a minute, wait a minute. Hold it, guys. I mean it."

At first, the band thought she was clowning—which she often did—so they half-continued to play until she really brought them to a halt by calling out to the floor manager to turn up the house lights.

Barbra joked with the audience, saying things like, "Hey, you're always lookin' at me, why don't I get a chance to see you?" Pointing to an older man at a table with a younger-looking blonde, she quipped, "Oh, she's not the one you brought here last week." The drummer hit the drums to help punctuate. The bass player and the pianist joined in. As she talked, Barbra began jerking and shifting parts of her body around. "Just trying to get some of these kinks out, you know?" The audience enjoyed her jokes and these new gyrations.

"Boy, what a day I had, I'm really bushed." The audience wasn't sure now what she was up to, because she began making strange sounds as she continued her unwinding movements. A few people laughed, and even the musicians started chuckling. But as she talked on, explaining some of the trials and tribulations of her day and telling anecdotes about the celebrities on the show with her, the trio realized that as funny as her stories were, the efforts to relieve the kinks in her body were quite serious. The musicians empathized with her, and changed from playing a series of comedic accompaniments to more sinuous and thoughtful chords and runs. The mood in the room changed as well. Here was a star performer revealing her tensions to an audience, demonstrating how to solve them, and being entertaining at the same time.

By now, Barbra was far along in her relaxation, half-hanging her limbs like the straw man in *The Wizard of Oz*, muttering soft but wildly elongated sounds from inside her. The pianist had begun a plaintive run that could easily lead to any number of ballads in Barbra's repertoire. The floor manager had caught on and slowly lowered the house lights. The bass player strummed evocatively. The drummer used his brush. The audience grew hushed.

Barbra moved a stool close to the piano, her arms dangling loosely as she lifted it from the floor. She climbed up on it, leaned her arms behind her and dropped her head back. In a few moments, a quiet but golden tone emanated from her throat. The sound was effortless, the resonances seemed to come from everywhere within her. She was singing one of her loveliest numbers, "When a Bee Lies Sleepin'."

Her head stayed back for almost a third of the song, but by the time she brought herself up and forward, her voice filled the room with rich, gorgeous sound. The musicians improvised new choruses.

By the end of the song, Barbra was radiating feelings connected with the song. It was as fresh and moving as anything she had ever done. The audience applauded as if they'd been granted a privilege.

By the end of the set, Barbra couldn't stop. Her final number was "Lover Come Back To Me." She took the last bars of that song into so many interpretations that it could have become a record on its own. The band was exhausted but happy from trying to keep up with her. The audience was on its feet stamping with excitement. Barbra looked exalted, flushed with energy and emotion. And this was the lady who barely an hour earlier was complaining how tired she was. By relaxing *into* her tiredness, she removed the blocks that had separated her inner being from her performing self.

Make the time to practice this relaxation exercise in full at least once a day. At other times, especially while actively engaged in regular activi-

ties, focus on only one portion of your body at a time, using the bands principle, and try to disengage any tensions you find in that area. In the market, while rolling your shopping cart through the aisles, relax from your knees down to your feet. While driving, relax your neck into your shoulders (without taking your eyes from the road, of course). When painting a kitchen, relax all the way down your back. And remember to add sounds as you do any of these relaxations. They can be sotto voce *so as not to disturb those around you, or they can be at full volume, depending on your surroundings. Then perhaps late that night, just before retiring, you may want to go through the entire exercise again. It will usually help soothe you to sleep.*

Inner relaxation is essential to achieve a condition of openness, of childlike availability—a state in which creativity can best flourish.

We're all looking for that release, that letting-go of the barriers that hold our realest expressions in. Relaxation, structured and maintained, will do that for you.

Remember, this is not a magic formula. Doing it once, twice, or even a few times won't permanently relieve you of your anxieties. It will, though, prevent your tensions from building up, day by day. And you'll be learning a way to help short-circuit your habitual patterns of repressing thoughts and feelings.

The more regularly you practice this relaxation exercise, the more it will benefit you.

As you continue to explore relaxation as a learned skill, try to keep these two principles in mind: 1) use the least amount of energy necessary for a given task, and 2) strive for an openness to express whatever sensations are then aroused. To fully engage your responses and your capacities to respond, you have to allow all feelings to arise, without judging which are "good" and which are "bad." Many of your responses will make you uncomfortable; so be it. Some of your responses will upset you; that's life. After all, this is how you grew up. As an infant, by admitting all your sensations, you accumulated rich and continuous experiences. Hopefully, as you grew older, you also learned that you had the right to choose which sensations you wished to avoid. But first you had to admit them. If you've forgotten that basic lesson in life, this procedure will help remind you.

Sense and Emotional Memories

One of the great performances in my experience was Alfred Lunt's in a Broadway production of Friedrich Dürrenmatt's *The Visit*. Lunt played Anton Schill, a long-time resident of a small town in Switzerland, who in his much-younger years had deflowered a young woman, Claire Wascher, then cast her aside. Shamed by what had happened to her, and taunted and harassed by the inhabitants, the young woman fled the town. As the play opens, the woman—now Claire Zachanassian, a multimillionairess—is just returning. The town is desperately poor, and the inhabitants now fawn upon their once-fallen flower, seeking any means to partake of some of her enormous wealth. She offers one, and only one, such opportunity: she will give the town prosperity if the townspeople will kill her former lover, Schill.

In the early stages of the play there is no mention of this possible gift. Everyone in the town is curious about Madame Zachanassian's visit. She seems affable; a little distant, but certainly not vindictive toward anyone. She even visits Schill and seems to want to spend time with him. He is at first uneasy, but her manner is reassuring. Only slowly do his suspicions grow, not from her, but from the gradual cooling and intrigues of his neighbors. By the end of the play, the entire town is mobilized, and when Schill seeks passage on a train to escape, the townspeople surround the station to kill him.

Lunt's choices of behavior for this role included a sequence of a slowly graduated constriction of his body from early on in the first act to a convulsive throwing-up against the wall of the station as the townspeople crowded in on him at the end of the play. His terror was unforgettable, totally riveting. I found myself almost unable to breathe during those last moments before he collapsed, he was so convincing. And I determined to find out what he had done to accomplish that sequence of terror.

A friend of his, who was also a friend of mine, told me. This friend was an actor as well, and his admiration for Lunt's accomplishments was just as fierce as mine. He went backstage after he had seen the play for the second time and asked Lunt what he had used to create the sequence. Lunt's response was, "Well, you know when you get scared you usually have to go to the bathroom. And if there is no relief possible, and the fear continues, your body contorts until you finally have to throw up." Well said, and incredibly well-executed.

I don't mean to suggest that Lunt literally threw up at every performance of the play; he acted it out, he behaved as his body would if it were unable to expel toxic material over that period of time.

Every human predicament and every human endeavor or action has finite physical details inherent in it that can be structured into a sequence of behavior.

We are all sensory creatures. Without continual input of sensory experience and accompanying personal associations, none of us would be able to function. Our astronauts-in-training in the late 1960s confirmed this fact. All the highly-skilled pilot/candidates underwent complex and often painful training. By their own accounts, they agreed that the most difficult test—and the only one they were unable to endure—was the sensory deprivation test.

One at a time, each astronaut, wearing a wet suit from head to toe to prevent actual contact with the water, was lowered into a very large tank of water heated to body temperature. Fastened underneath each man were pontoons that kept him on his back in a simulation of weightlessness. The sides of the tank were padded so that any accidental or intentional contact would barely be felt. All light was blocked from the chamber, as were all sounds and smells. Each trainee faced an environment devoid of outside sensory stimuli.

Each man tried to keep himself occupied in the black space. Some sang songs, some did verbal and mathematical problems, told themselves stories and jokes, called out lists of foods they'd eaten and films they'd seen; nothing worked for very long. Within eleven to fourteen hours, every one of these superbly trained, highly motivated men began to hallucinate so severely that the test had to be called off.

Disc jockeys doing telethons and scientists working on repetitive experiments over extended periods of time have been known to suffer hallucinations as well. Their energies and activities were too narrowly focused for them to maintain sensibility. They began to crack.

We are all aware that a blind person listens and hears far more acutely than a sighted one, that a deaf person will see and smell far more perceptively than an unimpaired person. There seems to be a natural ability and need to compensate for missing or lowered sensory receptivity.

We not only need to use our senses—we cannot live if they are all removed.

There is one other aspect of sensory experience worth stressing. A convention of ophthalmologists in the late 1950s put out a paper describing our human visual process this way: the images that we see pass through the mechanism of the eye and go on to the brain, where they become "tinged with memory." Some of the time, the process may be deliberate, such as when you pick out a present you are sure will elicit good feelings from the recipient, or when you are planning a dinner of favorite dishes that you know will please the guest. Other times, the process may be unconscious, or even illusory. Anyone who drives a car, for example, will on some occasion "see" a dead cat or dog run over on the road ahead and respond accordingly, but on closer approach, the animal turns out to be a pile of burned-off tire or a heap of cloth. I've had the experience, as have others, of grabbing a pot from a burner on the stove and cursing because it felt hot—then realizing the flame had never been turned on.

Myriad unconscious connections to past events and people are simply there, needing only the triggering release of the proper sensory stimulus. I still don't know why the smell of bacon and eggs makes me feel good. Or why a certain kind of light, just before dusk when the sky is relatively cloudless, fills me with a calm that is beyond the beauty of the colors around me.

Actors need to train and harness their sensory perceptions for a multitude of reasons. Most importantly, sensory perceptions are the control factors for all emotional responses. It is impossible for any of us to have an emotional response without a prior sensory stimulus, conscious or unconscious. We can have a visual impression of a loved one and a flow of warm feelings arises. Some of us hear the brass of a marching band, and we are stirred. All of us taste good food or wine, and our inner beings feel gratified. We can arouse these same responses by the memory of these sensory impressions—but it takes practice.

Sidney Poitier once expressed it this way in *American Film*: "I've always dipped into my own life, my own experiences. Because in the confines of it, I've had joy and I've had pain, I've had fears, and I've been courageous. There is something you want; once you know what, you just call on your memory bank and you've got it."

Pavlov proved the existence of conditioned sensory reflexes in his experiments with dogs. Whenever a bell was rung, the dogs would be fed. After a number of times, the dogs would salivate every time the bell was rung, whether there was food present or not.

The same is true of conditioning emotional responses to appropriate sensory stimuli. Once defined and practiced, we can stock a storehouse of varied sense memories of our individual experiences. With Pavlov, the sequence of the bell, then food, had to be repeated over a hundred times to guarantee the dogs' salivating. Let's give ourselves credit for a somewhat finer sensitivity than canines, and let's say that the exercises I'll outline should be repeated *a number of times* before any assured future response will take place.

Thousands and thousands of sensory experiences are part of everyone's lives by the time we are young adults. Some stay consciously part of our lives, some have to be rediscovered. When I had just been introduced to sensory work in an acting class and was excited by its prospects, I suddenly found myself almost blank on childhood objects and events. Whether because of an unconscious resistance to raising the memories of early experiences I feared might be terrible, or simply from lack of practice at reminding myself of earlier times, I seemed unable to remember my mother's cooking, my father's voice or manner, what our pet cat looked like, or even any birthday presents I had received.

For a while, I called my mother regularly—she was most available, and had been in charge of most of my early growing-up—and tried to make her remember enough details of events I'd been exposed to in order to trigger my own memories. (She never could understand those calls of mine, but she figured actors do peculiar things). Eventually she would tell me whatever she could remember, and bit by bit, event by event, I gradually recalled more on my own.

The floods of emotion that were released as I practiced reviewing these experiences were dumbfounding. It was as if as an adult I had hardly touched the emotional resources within me. For months, my acting work was almost drowned in these waves of feeling, which had to be given their own way for me to gain any real use of them. It was through systematic trial-and-error contact with these memories that I became a more accessible, emotional actor.

I am not claiming that sense memories are the only path to emotional life. There is no question that great actors have always been able to enter into the emotional lives of their roles purely by responding to the character's plight in the text, or by imagining similar situations in their own lives—*some of the time.* There is also no question that great actors, since the beginning of recorded theatrical history, sometimes needed the added stimulus of a personal experience to fully invigorate a performance.

It was Konstantin Stanislavski who became the first codifier of the processes by which some of these great moments in performances occurred. After much observation of great acting from all over the world, he discovered that memorable sequences were often achieved through the actor's use of actual experiences, and he was able to define the procedures by which these experiences were unleashed. He termed them *sense memory* and *emotional memory.*

A *sense memory* entails the use of one or more of our five senses at a time to define a single known object or stimulus: the

view at a beach, the bark of a dog, the smell of cut grass, the
taste of an orange, the touch of a summer breeze.

It's usually easiest to begin a sense memory recall by using
either a smell or a sound. We don't tend to pay as much attention
to these senses as sight or touch or taste, so the exploration
becomes more of an adventure.

*Pick the smell of a rose. Close your eyes, breathe easily and regularly,
give in to a state of relaxation, with no expectations or demands as to
what should take place, then leave yourself open to the mental image
of the rose you are trying to smell. You may, and probably will, find
your mind tossing various rose images at you: yellow, red, single-bud-
ded or multi-budded, in a garden or in a shop, in someone's hands or
in a vase. Let yourself sift among the images until you settle on one
more than any others. And if not, choose one. Begin to smell what is
actually around you where you sit. See if any of these real smells
comes close to the smell of the particular rose that you chose.
Gradually leave off the smells around you (don't suppress them, don't
reject them, simply leave them in abeyance) and allow the rose more
and more room in your sensory imagination. You may begin to
believe you actually smell this rose; most often, you will not. But you
will find that the sensory impression you've created does influence
your feelings. And that's the real point of this exercise:* to awaken sensations tinged with memories. *It is those memories that contain the
emotions.*

*It's quite easy to establish practice exercises of your own. Begin with
any handy object or activity, such as your morning cup of coffee.
Smell the coffee, feel its heat on your face, the heft of the mug in your
hand. Slowly, almost as slowly as in a slow-motion film, sip the coffee,
feel its heat and wetness and its taste inside your mouth. Try to follow
its progress down your throat and into your stomach. Define where
and when you lose its heat and taste. Sip again. And repeat the inves-
tigation for several minutes. Then go about your business.*

*Later in the day, find a quiet location, relax, and pantomime the
activity of the morning, slowly. Take a lot more time than you usually
do to drink. Remind yourself of all the sensory details you can.*

*That evening, or whenever you have time later, repeat the remem-
bering procedure.*

The next morning, confirm your sensory memories of the activity by drinking another cup of coffee, prepared the same way.

After a couple of days, as you pantomime the activity and try to re-experience it, ask yourself what other memories of drinking coffee might occur to you: other times, other places, with other people. And soon, as you continue practicing the exercise, the imaginary act of drinking coffee will regularly activate sensations and feelings associated with many other occasions.

Don't try to predict or presume what experiences may be stirred by any of these memories. Try to accept whatever feelings arise. We all know how easy and natural it is to laugh at the memory of a disastrous hiking trip made years earlier, or to be saddened at the memory of a wonderful romance that ended long ago. Events do change in our remembrances. Either we change them consciously, because of how we currently wish to think of ourselves, or it's our psyche's unconscious way of dealing with those memories. In any case, truth is only truth as it occurs, not how we wish it to be. So it is with a sense or emotional memory. Train yourself to accept its own results. If you want to achieve a different result, it's easy enough: just use another memory.

I believe that for every emotional or physical necessity in acting a role, there are comparative sensory experiences available to the actor. If you don't drink, but need to do a drunk scene, remember donating blood—only instead of removing one pint, imagine the nurse accidentally removing two or three. How might your body then react? Or what about getting out of bed after a prolonged high fever? Just take away the element of weakness, but keep the lightheadedness, the sense of being off-balance, and the shakiness, and you will come very close to a state of drunkenness.

(After my first attempt at a drunk scene in a class, the teacher asked me if I drank. I answered no, so he said "You should!" On my way home, I bought a fifth of bourbon, then sat in my living room and drank half the bottle in fifteen minutes. All that I remember is passing out and waking up hours later, headachy and nauseous. I don't recommend this technique to anyone.)

If your character suffers from migraine headaches and you've never had one, remind yourself of a toothache or a severe pain somewhere else in your body. Re-create it sensorially, then imagine that same condition in your forehead. Or perhaps you'd respond better if you thought of a large vise applied to your head—that could lead to quite a headache.

A young man, an Irish actor in one of my classes in the early 1960s, had great difficulty caressing his attractive partner in a love scene they had prepared. He had only recently come to the States, and in Ireland young lovers were not demonstrative, especially in front of others. He even had difficulty kissing her goodbye. With his partner beside him, I asked him what kind of fruit he particularly relished during the hot summers. He said his favorite was peaches, but he hardly ever had any; they were too expensive. I asked what degree of ripeness the peaches had to be to satisfy him the few times he'd had them. He described a very slight darkening of the skin—not browning, which would be over-ripe—just a deepening of the yellows and reds until they almost joined colors. It wouldn't be too firm, it would have a slight give to the touch. And the smell would be exotic, heady. He glowed a little as his memory and imagination merged to create a perfectly satisfying peach. I then asked him to imagine taking a bite. He mimed the peach. He defined the texture and the touch and the smell, then bit slowly into it. He almost moaned with pleasure. I told him to try to imagine a basket, a good-sized basket, full of those perfect peaches that he was free to eat at any time. Or just fondle. Or smell. His hands went out to his imaginary basket, his face was alive with anticipated pleasures. As he became engrossed with his fruit and those pleasures, I asked him to turn to his acting partner and treat her as he would the peaches. What a great love scene ensued! He turned beet red doing it, but he did it, and so did his partner. By the time they were kissing, I could swear she was eating peaches, too.

I was not only a classmate of Geraldine Page's, I also became her part-time coach for her role in Tennessee Williams' *Sweet Bird of Youth*. Her character was a once magnificent, now faded silent-film star well down on her luck, but with an unquenchable desire to live fully. She was also still quite sexy.

Geraldine, for whatever unknown reasons, found herself inhibited in this area. I asked if she'd ever been around a cat in heat.

She said indeed she had. I told her to think of the movements the cat goes through at such a time, the lowering of the back and midsection, the raising of the hindquarters; I asked her to remember the sounds the creature makes, the quality of its voice as it invites a male partner. Her eyes glinted with recognition. I suggested that every once in a while, during everyday activities, arbitrarily and subtly, she was to arch her rump, stretch through her back into her neck, and let her voice out with the quality of the cat in heat—while she showered, prepared a meal, talked on the telephone, lounged on her sofa. In no time at all, Geraldine vibrated mischievously with this new-found sensuality. You can still see it in her film performance.

When Barbra Streisand was fifteen years old, she was still unknown as a singer, and certainly unknown as an actress. She was untutored, ignorant of any acting techniques, but fervent about learning all she could. She had no income, so I placed her on scholarship. She cajoled me into more acting lessons even on our bus rides to and from my studio.

After a year of classes and coaching, her acting was improving wondrously. I cast her in a one-act play, Christopher Fry's *A Phoenix Too Frequent*, which was to be part of a showcase program I directed.

Early rehearsals were a pleasure. The three actors in the play enjoyed working with each other and me, and the work was specific and rewarding. Until—we reached the point where the emotional lives of the characters needed more defining. Barbra was playing the serving girl to a wealthy, recently-widowed lady. The play is set in the tomb of the deceased master of the house in ancient Greece, where custom has dictated that the widow must now take her own life. This she seems willing to do, albeit not enthusiastically. Custom also dictates that the widow is not only allowed but encouraged to take a favored servant with her, in this case, Barbra's character.

The play is a comedy, though it may not sound like one. The dialogue and relationships are witty and satiric, but that didn't mean the circumstances should be played without real emotion (as is true of all well-played comedies). In fact, I determined that the serving girl should be even more desolate and self-lamenting than her mistress. After all, the serving girl was still practically a child, and had just begun to live.

In one particular sequence in the play when the widow, tired and forlorn, has fallen asleep, the serving girl has a monologue in which she despairs of ever seeing her beloved kitchen and boyfriends again. I felt Barbra should shed tears during this speech. She didn't disagree; she just didn't know how to do it.

As I tried various acting techniques to help her realize the emotional distress we agreed upon for the character, I began to realize that as much as I thought I knew about Barbra, I really knew little of her sadder emotional life. She had blockaded herself over the years from any form of self-pity, including crying. Tears seemed unknown to her.

I tried sense memories and emotional memories, with no success. I began to improvise imaginary situations which I hoped would elicit emotional responses of the tearful kind. I tried terrifying situations—falling off a boat in the dark and being menaced by sharks, coming home at night and being threatened by a mugger. I tried sad ones—little kids in trouble, needing to be rescued. I tried everything I could think of for hours and then more hours over a period of days, but nothing came close to what we were looking for. Performance time was approaching.

I contacted friends who were fellow acting teachers and fellow actors, discussed my dilemma with Barbra, listened to as much advice as I thought practical, and tried every new suggestion offered to me. None worked. I gave up and actually began to hope for an artistic miracle.

The day before our first and only dress rehearsal, which was to be followed by a single weekend of performances, Barbra and I were having a light lunch together, just the two of us, before meeting the other actors. She had many questions about another actor's performance she'd seen recently on stage, and about other actors' work in classes she'd been observing. It occurred to me that for at least the past six months, these were practically the only subjects we'd been discussing.

I moved into questions of my own: "Do you miss living in Brooklyn, or seeing your sister or brother? Have you thought yet about ever having children of your own? Or even a husband?

What kind of man might he be?" Despite her wariness, the questions gradually shifted her into a kind of receptivity. I suddenly thought of a question that seemed to hold even larger potential for her: "What do you think you'd do if you couldn't act?"

Expecting a long, silent, troubled response, I was floored when she said immediately, "Open a bakery shop."

She was delighted at my weak reply, "You're kidding."

"I've always wanted to have a bakery where I could make any breads I liked," she continued, "pastries for every occasion, all designed by me. I love the smell of bakeries. I love the look of bakeries. I could spend my whole life in a bakery!" The undiminished glee and adventurousness in her eyes and voice inspired me.

"What do you mean, for occasions? Whose?"

"Mine, yours, anybody's. For a birthday, or graduation, anything I felt like."

"Well, for instance, what kind of concoction would you pick for your own birthday?"

"If it was a regular or a special one?" she asked. "I mean, if it was, like, my sixteenth birthday or eighteenth?"

"Okay, let's say it's your twenty-first." (She'd already passed her sixteenth.) "What would you make for that one?"

Barbra launched into a description of a massive, two-foot-high, multilayered mixture of creams and fudge and jams in between fluffy cake tastes of incredible variety. As she described one ingredient after another, her hands began demonstrating how these ingredients blended and the decorative motifs she would use. She pantomimed an entire cake before my eyes, shifting from pleasure to pleasure and ending almost in a state of ecstasy.

When the last detail had been arranged, including a figure of herself in whipped cream at the very top, I exclaimed, "That's gorgeous. I could eat it right here."

Her eyes clouded. "You can't have any, it's mine. I made it for my birthday." I began to sing "Happy Birthday" to her. I was moved by what she had done and admitted about herself, and expressed my feelings as I sang. I began to tear up a little, and so did she.

"All right," she said when I finished, "you can have a slice. That was very nice."

I was still smiling at her as she very carefully, but with real feeling, cut me a slice of her imagined creation. It was a substantial slice. "Thank you," I said, and reached my hands out for it.

She beamed at me. "I hope you like it."

"Of course I will," I said, and then suddenly acted as if the cake had slipped from my hands and dropped on the floor.

"Ohh nooo," she wailed, "no, no, nooo!" Tears welled up in her eyes.

"I'm sorry, I'm so sorry," I said desperately, playing into her tears.

"Why did you do that? Why did you drop my cake?" She was really crying now. I repeated over and over how sorry I was. She was very forlorn and hurt for quite a while, but we eventually made peace. She continued to ask why I had done that, but I didn't tell her. I knew that she knew it all had to do with the play.

The following day, before the evening's dress rehearsal, I called our stage manager aside, gave him a dollar, and asked him to go out to one of the nearby good restaurants and buy the most luscious-looking whipped-cream piece of pastry available (in those days, a dollar could buy a very expensive piece of pastry). I then picked out a particular line of Barbra's dialogue in the script and told him that as she spoke that line he was to stand in the wings off to the right of the stage, and facing her he was to gobble down that piece of pastry, enjoying every bite of it. He, of course, wanted to know why, and I answered, "You'll know why when you see what happens to her." And I swore him to secrecy about the plan.

I found Barbra. On the pretext of changing a piece of staging, I asked her to turn to her right as she delivered that particular line of dialogue—the line that was the beginning of her lament over being too young to die and not being able to stand the loss of her pots and pans, and lovers.

That evening, it was hard for me to focus on anything else. At the proper moment, when Barbra turned stage right, I think I stopped breathing. Then the most outrageous caterwauling noise rose out of her as she clearly saw that gorgeous piece of pastry being eaten up out of the audience's view. She cried, she laughed, she expressed disbelief and loss. She continued, as the terrific young actress that she was, to allow those surprised feelings to surge through her as she continued her speech. The audience roared with laughter, was moved, and ended up applauding her performance before she even finished her monologue. Each night we repeated the process. Another dollar, another piece of pastry, another off-stage eating, and another superior performance. Barbra was a good enough actress to allow herself to respond to that made-up offstage activity, without it ever separating her from the flow of the play.

I mentioned an actor facing death at the beginning of this chapter. I once had a suicide sequence to play at the Actors Studio. One of my all-time favorite writers was J.D. Salinger. He'd never written a play, but several of his short stories had actable sequences without any adaptation necessary. "For Esmé—with Love and Squalor" was one of those.

A young American soldier is stationed in England during World War II. While training in a pre-invasion course directed by British Intelligence in Devon, he's drawn by the sounds of a choir practice. He watches one thirteen-year-old girl (Esmé) in particular, and finds her voice especially lovely. After practice, he has the opportunity to talk to the precocious girl and her brother in a tea room. He notices a large watch, a man-sized watch, the girl is wearing. She tells him it was her father's; he was killed in the war, as was her mother. It's the one memento she has of her father's. The soldier is very taken with Esmé's innocence, and she with him. They exchange addresses and promise to write.

Flash forward: the soldier is sent into gruesome combat. The Allies win the war. He suffers a nervous breakdown, is sent to a hospital. He feels his life is useless, and everyone around him inhuman and unthinking. He relates to no one, and it is crushing him. Alone, while contemplating ending his life, he notices a package from someone whose name is unfamiliar. He opens it and finds a letter and a gift from Esmé. She has sent the only thing she had, her father's watch, because she thinks it will help him. Her gesture restores his belief in human relationships, and in the last line of the story he lays his head down and falls ecstatically asleep.

The story touched deep chords within me. I felt I could act anything in it just by reading it over and over, except his facing suicide. That was something out of my experience or imagination at
that time. I couldn't quite comprehend what would make anyone
take his life, unless perhaps an incurable, terrible disease like cancer. But this, it seemed to me, was a different kind of hopelessness.

I had already scheduled myself to act an improvisation based
on the last scene in the story at the Actors Studio (usually you had
to do that weeks in advance), and I was getting extra anxious as
the time approached. I discussed what I was stuck on with several
actor friends, but no one's suggestions seemed helpful, and I
didn't dare go to Strasberg. Finally, I sat myself down and made
myself try to define the kind of state someone might have to be in
to want to kill oneself, short of having a deadly illness. Several
ideas went by until the thought of feeling all alone in the world
struck. Totally alienated. Not the loneliest time in one's life, but
the alone-est. That hit something in me. I'd had many awfully
alone times as a child, so I began reminding myself of several.
But as I relaxed and made myself feel open to their possibilities,
they seemed too young, too naive as experiences to use as a basis
for the short-story scene. And then I remembered a time when I
had been overseas as a soldier, had gotten into deep trouble with
my commanding officer, and had been ostracized by every single
member of my company for weeks. I'd never felt so alone and
helpless in my adult life.

Sensorially, I recalled the barracks room where we lived and
slept. Forty beds, forty wall and foot lockers, twenty windows,
two wood-burning stoves. Dark wood walls and floors, army reg-
ulation blankets, stoves black. One doorway, stairs down to the
main floor. Men's voices always. Truck motors continuously running (we were a supply unit). Until nighttime. Then the men's
voices, their showering noises, and the recreation room's piano
sounds began to fade as the men all left the barracks for their
night out. Several truck engines joined by a few jeeps roared into
gear, then disappeared down the road. All gone, except for me,
night after night.

When I did the scene, I began where the soldier in the story
was finally left alone. I set the stage like his room: one bed, one

desk, one door, a stack of mail including a package I had wrapped and addressed with the name of the character in the story, inside of which I had put my own young son's Mickey Mouse wristwatch, and an exact copy of the letter written by Esmé. There was also a typewriter.

I mentally surrounded myself with a sensory re-creation of my barracks room. As I went through the actual action described in the story, I imagined my barracks room with all those fellow soldiers preparing to leave. Salinger wrote about the soldier being left alone; I thought of me being left alone, the sounds of those voices, footsteps, trucks and jeeps moving further and further away. What I didn't anticipate, and may not have remembered, was the awful silence in which I was left. I moved to the doorway I had set up, listening for the sound of anyone still in the building. As I opened the door wider, the better to hear, it squeaked.

I became fascinated by that one sound. I swung the door back and forth, back and forth, I don't know how many times. I only remember how soothed it made me feel. A truck rolled by in the street outside the Studio. I turned toward it, as my stomach jumped, but it faded very quickly. I looked about the room I had set up. I kept comparing it to the barracks in my memory. The room onstage seemed so small. I began to pace it, making my footsteps harder and harder on the floor as I walked, building up sound. But this noise felt harsh, and my head began to shake from side to side, as a deep moan came up within me. The typewriter came into focus. I rushed to it, inserted a sheet of paper, the noise of the roller and the clicks of the apparatus felt good, alive. I started typing not words, but letters. It was the sounds of the keys striking that I was really after. I tried to make music with the keys, faster and faster, but just as I came close to a melody, the keys became locked, the instrument jammed. I couldn't pry the keys loose. I remembered the soldier's next action in the story: going through his mail. Hurriedly (I was getting extremely agitated), I raced through the pile, checking return addresses (which I had written out to myself) until I came to the package tied with string.

I stared at its return address, and allowed myself quick flashes of the meeting of the soldier with Esmé in the story. My skin started to prickle. My heart seemed to be beating loudly enough for me to hear it. I broke the string, but it made barely a sound. I tore open the paper, which made much more satisfying crackling noises. My fingers curled in between the pieces as I unraveled the paper from the box inside. Holding some of the papers between my fingers for the noises they added, I lifted the lid, and found the watch. I picked it up, then saw the note folded underneath. I dropped the paper in my other hand and unfolded the note.

I read every word very slowly. By the time I finished, I was crying. What Esmé had written was so beautiful, so thoughtful. To have sent the one precious memento left in her life was a gift beyond comprehension. I stared at the Mickey Mouse watch in front of me, images of my own son mixing and blending with Salinger's description of Esmé and her younger brother. I felt cared about. I began to believe in the decency of humankind. It was overwhelming. I wound the watch. The stem created a tiny gear-like rhythm very faintly. I held the watch to my ear as its mechanism whirred to life. It was the sweetest sound I could have imagined at that time. I put the watch into my mouth, the better to have it resonate all through me. Then, "ecstatically," I laid my head down to sleep. I felt utterly at one with Salinger's soldier.

This was an exercise, an improvisation without benefit of a director or the approval of the author. I submit it as an example of an actor's exploration. But it was a memorable experience for me because everyone at the Studio agreed it was my finest work to date. I couldn't have done it without sense memories.

Once you have established a body of sense memory exercises, it's time to begin mixing them. Combine your experience of drinking a cup of coffee with hearing the sound of a childhood friend's voice. Or the smell of your grandmother's perfume while you drink a glass of milk. Or the taste of a favorite food while lying under a shade tree. Pick one of the sensory tasks to be more inner, the other to be more outwardly available.

And when you have begun to master these simple combinations, add others and/or make mixtures that interact in opposites: Use a pleasurable sound—your mother's voice (or your father's or a friend's) when you were very young and sick in bed and she comforted you.

Remind yourself of the room, yourself lying in bed, your soreness, then the look of the person, and then her voice. As you give way to the person's soothing, hum a military march. Try to maintain contact with the qualities of the person's voice even as the march seems to drown it out. Let the voice affect your humming, let the humming disturb the memory of the voice. Let the humming go. Bring it back in. Let it take over, lose the voice. Mix them and match them. And whatever happens to you, let it happen.

Here's another mixture. Remember sunning yourself at the beach: the sense of space, sky, vista of sand, the time of day. Leave out other people, just you and a beach you're familiar with. Recall your body stretched out on a blanket or on the sand itself, close your eyes and with your mind trace out the effects sunshine would have on you as you first lay out. Begin with your face, then move on down. Think of gradually lengthening the time you are exposed. Imagine increasing perspiration on different parts of your body, including your back, the buildup of heat, the glow of your skin as you extend the time even further.

When you are well into the reconstruction, consider a cobweb descending on you, all over. Don't try to motivate how it might get there, just add it to the sun and the heat. Alternate these experiences. And sing a song. You can even use the military march I suggested in the previous exercise just to see how this mixture will affect it. Mix them and match them. Just as we do in life. There is no such thing as only one color of emotion that we feel at a given time. That only happens in cartoons—or with bad acting.

As you gather these sensory experiences through trial and error, you will find some extremely vivid and moving. Try using these as the basis for your feelings and behavior as you rehearse monologues and scenes. Use a combination of outer and inner sense memories. Have them counter each other; let one be more warming and sentimental, the other more abrasive and disturbing. When they are both in focus and affecting you, add the words of your monologue or dialogue instead of a song. Let the sensory stimuli weave in and out of the thoughts and feelings expressed in the script. You will soon see the advantages of using sensory tasks to explore your material.

You will also see that certain material requires an extended emotional response, or a sudden, traumatic kind: a young woman facing death by fire (Joan of Arc), a man being informed that his lover was killed on the job by a berserk employee, a woman being told that she has just delivered twins. For events like these, an *emotional memory* can be invaluable.

An emotional memory—sometimes called *affective memory* or *emotional recall*—uses all five senses to reconstruct a one-time event: receiving a memorable gift, an especially difficult time with a dentist, the birth of a child, a first-time trip to the country (if you lived in the city).

Among many of our finest acting teachers from the 1930s to the present, there have been heated disagreements as to the value of emotional memories. Lee Strasberg and Stella Adler became real enemies primarily over this issue. Lee clung to his belief that emotional memory was the single most valuable component of an actor's equipment. Stella, who verified Stanislavski's original use of emotional memory in conversations with Stanislavski directly, insisted it was only one small part of any actor's training.

It's a moot point. Emotional memories have been and will continue to be used by actors everywhere. Some actors, especially in contemporary naturalistic-tending theater, film, and television, will utilize emotional memories more than others. They really should be used more often by actors doing Shakespeare and Eugene O'Neill, or even Chekhov and Ibsen, where sustained passions are essential. Because whether you use them to trigger specific emotional responses in performance or not, emotional memories are invaluable in the creation of a highly vulnerable and psychically open state, a state in which your emotions and intuitions become easily stirred by the material itself.

From the earliest times of recorded theatrical history, there have been examples of actors using personal experiences to ignite their characters' responses on stage. In a funeral oration, a classic Greek actor came on stage with the ash-filled urn of his recently deceased son to spur himself on.

I remember once being told of a memorable scene in a play called *The Bluebird*, directed by the renowned Russian director Vachtangov, a student of Stanislavski's. In *The Bluebird*, a young princess is informed that her lover, who has been imprisoned, now faces probable execution. Vachtangov decided that instead of a farewell note to her lover, the princess should send her tears. In the production, the princess summoned her courtier, bade him remove his hat, lamented her poor lover's fate, and then cried her loving tears into the hat, which the courtier carried to her lover. The actress used a personal emotional experience to stir herself to tears and, with the director's help and vision, she cried openly enough to have her tears drop into a hat.

Recently, I appeared in a film made for television, starring a very popular television comedy series actress who had a crying scene to do. We rehearsed it a couple of times but no tears appeared.

The director, being nicely supportive, asked if the actress would like to be squirted (by a harmless chemical lightly dropped into the eyes, which causes tearing—and which, by the way, is used frequently for crying scenes in TV and films). She responded by saying that this was a really serious film and she'd like to take a shot at it on her own when we did an actual take.

I appreciated that, and looked forward to her reaction. The director called for the camera to roll, and off we went. Sure enough, just about the time the script called for tears, the actress turned her back to me—which was part of the staging—and as my character continued to provoke her, she wheeled on me, eyes brimming, voice cracked with emotion. But all of a sudden she broke off, rattled, and said "Sorry, I forgot the line."

The director called "Cut!" and immediately approached us. He was quite pleased. But the actress was remorseful. "I'm sorry," she said. "You know, the crying had nothing to do with my lines, so I couldn't remember them. Let me try it again so I can get used to it."

Here was an actress with at least twenty years of experience in television who had never known how to adapt her own experiences to acting, who was now apologizing for trying to use something personal to herself. I was astounded, and sympathetic. The poor lady simply didn't know. Remaining ignorant of the process of emotional memory is limiting for an actor, both artistically and practically.

In the beginning, an emotional memory cannot be hurried. You should allow up to forty-five minutes to fully engage yourself in one (but it will be a fascinating forty-five minutes). Later, when you've mastered the techniques of both sense and emotional memory, and have used them in actual rehearsals and performances, you'll find quicker stepping stones to any response you want to awaken. It will become your pleasure to use these tools, wherever, whenever, and however you wish—like a painter who has mastered the palette and then needs only a conception. The use of emotional memory becomes a triumph of skill and craftsmanship that will ultimately allow any actor to engage the full range of his or her emotional life toward the creation of life for a character.

Let me stress that until you have mastered this technique, you should practice this exercise only in the company of others—actor friends perhaps, or someone you can count on to be an objective presence for you, to help keep you from straying into subjective reactions.

Remember, your senses have been in use for many years. Now, for the purpose of an emotional memory, you are simply going to arrange them in a given order to construct a singular event.

There is no danger of going too far or losing control when doing an emotional memory. The fact that you've chosen to explore the event and are using a continuous listing of your sensory impressions to structure the memory will govern you, no matter how powerful the emotions raised. However, it's important that you begin your explorations with relatively untraumatic events—nothing like the death of a loved one or a maiming accident. It's also important to understand that any personal experience or event can feel traumatic at the time it happened (just watch any child lose a favorite toy). Try first to choose what you consider to be happy, cheerful, even silly one-time events. Many of them will turn out to be unsettling enough in their own ways. *Choose only incidents that happened at least five years ago.* Anything more recent tends to slip and slide in our memory banks, and leads to too many variations in our emotional responses.

All right, enough discussion. How do you actually do an emotional memory?

You start as you would when practicing a sense memory. Get yourself a chair with a firm back. Sit, breathe, relax, make sounds, then close your eyes (merely to help you focus; later, you can work with them open). Now, pick an event—let's say your first (and possibly last) blind date. Most of us have had one of those. Consider which moment you might call the climax *of the event: perhaps the first sight of your stranger-for-the-evening; perhaps one outrageous or ridiculous moment during the date; or perhaps it was the relieving final good-night as your partner disappeared from view. I'll choose the first example for the sake of illustration.*

The climax of this blind date event will be the moment in which you finally see the person you've been told about. In your mind's eye, move yourself back in time to approximately three minutes before this climax. It doesn't have to be exact. Mull over where you were at this three-minutes-earlier-time, what you were in the midst of doing, and any sights, sounds, smells, tastes, or touches of which you might have been aware. Let some of these various sensory details percolate around, and as they do, remember to check your breathing and your relaxation, and make low-decibel but open throat sounds to make sure your voice is ready to express whatever occurs.

You should stay seated during this entire forty-odd minutes. You will shift portions of your body dozens of times, but you should remind yourself to use your vocal capacities to channel all feelings and sensations that ensue. You may yell, you may perspire, you may feel woozy, or you may feel tingling in all your limbs. Your task is to keep yourself in that chair and let your voice carry everything—just as a newborn does.

After a minute or two of ruminating and checking your body and voice, with your eyes still closed, describe out loud, using the first person "I," the basic elements immediately around you in your memory, such as:

"I'm on a street in the middle of an area of two-story houses. Many trees. Driveways. The time is early evening. The sky is mostly clear. The temperature is comfortable, I guess around seventy degrees. Most of the houses have lights inside. Some also have porch lights. There's a little bit of a breeze, but very little smell in the air. But the air feels clear, fresh. I'm wearing a suit, kind of a grayish blue, a shirt and tie, both recently cleaned. And a relatively new pair of black shoes, freshly polished over an hour ago. A bus, the bus I arrived on, is just pulling away behind me. I can hear its engine and gears. There is a regular

flow of traffic facing me and coming from behind me..." (Whenever
you feel thoroughly involved, open your eyes.)

Now start the action *as if you were in a slow-motion film. For every
one of the three minutes of action that lead to the climax, you will
spend almost fifteen minutes in sensory descriptions:*

*"I am walking down the middle of a sidewalk, looking toward the
houses on my left, trying to make out numbers. I'm moving quickly. I
can feel the hard pavement under my feet. I can hear the sound of my
shoes in contact with the concrete. I still hear the sounds of traffic
though I'm not looking at the street. Most of the houses have porches.
The numbers I'm looking for are marked alongside the front door, or
sometimes on a porch pole. I don't remember most of the numbers, but
they're close to the one I'm looking for. My body is relatively cool, but I
feel a slight dampness in my armpits. As I walk I lift my arms away
from my sides to air them out. My breathing is tight, pressed. I can feel
myself sigh every once in a while to relieve the pressure..."*

Speak in a firm voice, allowing any bodily sensation to enter into
your tone. Pause frequently to double-check your breathing, various
portions of your body for tension, and the kind of sounds you're
making.

*"...The only sounds I hear are still from traffic. I don't taste any-
thing. The temperature is still cool. My stride is steady. I'm beginning
to feel stirrings in my stomach, little jumps. I keep looking at the house
numbers. I'm passing trees, lawns, there's a bicycle on a porch. I don't
remember its color. Or if it was a boy's bike or a girl's. The houses all
look dark, because it's evening. Everything looks mostly dark. The
street is lit, though, but I don't remember from what kind of street
lamps. There are a few cooking odors in the air like...I can't recall any
in particular, I just remember there were some. Probably like soups or
meat cooking. My armpits seem wetter now. I'm slowing my walk
because I can feel myself pressing forward. I'm stopping the walk. I'm
standing still. My body feels shivery. I'm not sure, but my shirt feels wet
in the back now. My face is starting to feel tight. I'm closing my eyes
and I can feel myself sighing. Really deep sighs. I'm stretching my
cheek muscles, and the muscles around my mouth. My mouth feels
dry now. I'm swallowing. As I stretch and sigh, I feel ripples of shivers
spread out from my stomach and chest into my arms. I just felt a couple of twitches in each leg. My feet now feel very tight in my shoes. I'm*

stretching one foot around in my shoe, my right one. Now I'm doing
the same with my left. My face feels even tighter. I'm getting very dry in
the mouth..."

What I'm describing is a continuing verbalization of a mixture of
all the areas of sensory detail as the action of moving from the bus stop
to my date's house takes place. Wherever there is a lapse of memory
(like the inability to recall the cooking odors), just say you don't
remember—you may pick it up later. But do place your focus on all
five senses, regardless of which one becomes most vivid. And keep the
action slowly moving forward until the moment of being greeted by
your date at the door of his or her house.

Notice that not once during the recall did I try to describe any
emotional or subjective reactions I felt. I never said, "I'm feeling
anxious" or "silly," or "the houses were ugly," or "the cooking
smells were wonderful." Verbalize *only in physical terms*: colors,
shapes, sizes, smells, sounds, tastes, touches. They hold the emotional fiber of our experiences. They are the means that will
release them. You must will yourself to use objective descriptions
of what any person on that street would have seen or smelled or
heard that night. Obviously, only you would have the exact sensations your body felt at that time, but you have to stay just as
objective about those sensations as you do about the physical
details that surround you.

After completing this approach to the blind-date experience,
you can vary the emotional content of the event by choosing a different climax, say, during the date or at the end of it. Then move
back in time three selected minutes from this new climax point.

If the memory of the event seems provocative, has in it interesting and risible emotional content, repeat it a few times. If it
seems discardable, let it go. You'll find plenty of others to draw
upon that will be loaded with richer responses.

When you first enter this emotional recall life, it may feel as if a
long-standing dam is suddenly giving way inside, and that your
darkest restricted feelings are forcing their way out first. People
tend to cry and rage at even the warmest, happiest memories.
Some of that can be because your deeper, more painful emotions
have been fighting longest and hardest to be expressed. Some of

it can happen because you no longer have many pleasurable experiences in your life, and you may cry out of self-pity or frustration. As you continue the process, the emotional forces within you will balance themselves out and you can traffic among them more objectively.

To encourage this balancing to come about more quickly, I have two suggestions. Once you've grown accustomed to reconstructing several emotional memories and have brought them to climax, say after a half dozen or so, the next time you find yourself in one that saddens and upsets you, somewhere past halfway through the recall, make yourself tell a joke—the worse the joke is, the better. Leave off the verbalization of the memory, but continue the sensory details and action in your head while you tell the joke out loud to whoever is in the room with you. Then verbally continue on with the upsetting emotional memory. Now it will be colored by the strangeness and unexpectedness of the joke-telling, and help bring about a wonderful mixture of emotions that brighten and vivify you.

I saw an example of this in a play on Broadway, James Baldwin's *Amen Corner.* It starred Beah Richards, a beautifully gifted actress, and was directed by Frank Silvera, a multitalented actor-director. Beah's character was a deeply religious woman who was living with her teenage son in Harlem. After many years of impoverishment, she had become the head of her own church. During the action of the play, her estranged husband dies, her son leaves her, and her congregation turns its back on her.

In the final scene of the play, Beah blew into her apartment as if a wind was at her back. She reeled about her kitchen, buffeted and beaten by the emotional and psychological forces that seemed about to destroy her, when all of a sudden she began to laugh—a rousing, thrilling peal of laughter ran through her body. She opened her arms, head uplifted, and laughed at the heavens. The audience exploded with relief. We all knew that this woman would survive and finally overcome. It was a gorgeous sequence of acting.

Someone I knew asked Beah how she had arrived at this great crying-laughing, uplifting ending. She said that she and Frank

Silvera had discussed the need to end the play on an upbeat sequence for her character, but given the awful circumstances in the woman's life, she couldn't do anything but cry her heart out. During one of the next rehearsals, when Beah arrived at that final sequence, and was being blown about by the demons tearing at her, Frank interrupted her.

"Beah, keep doing what you're doing, but listen to me..."

She quieted her sobs. Her body vibrated with feelings, but she listened.

"I want to tell you a little story." His voice was very gentle. "There was this lady, very poor lady, lived in this fourth floor walk-up. Electricity just about to be shut off, couldn't pay the bills. No hot water. Pipes all leaking. Her husband had been laid off for weeks, was sick now, couldn't get out of bed. And her boy had just been put in jail from a drug bust.

"Doorbell rings, she leans her head out the door and yells, 'Who is it?'

Man's voice calls back, 'Garbage.'

'Bring it on up,' she wails!'"

Beah was galvanized with laughter, and Frank simply said, "Now go on with the scene."

That's what she did from then on. In the midst of the darkest responses to her character's plight, Beah quickly told herself that old story of Frank's, then went on with the scene. It created a stunning illumination of the woman's character and soul.

Another suggestion: try an opposite mixture of the kind I just described. When you are thoroughly involved in an emotional-memory incident that raises warm, funny, generous feelings in you, make yourself retell a painful event. Don't drop the pleasurable incident, just park it while you tell this other short tale. Then as the sad, hurtful feelings come up in you, move yourself back into the original event. Let your emotions mix. Then try bringing those mixed feelings to a piece of material you are working on. Or a song. Or even a story from the newspapers or a magazine that made an impression on you. See what happens when the two independent forces are allowed to merge—how the words of your monologue, or the lyrics of the song, or the verbalized details of the newspaper story take on another life when stirred with your mixed emotional memory. It's often more engaging than when the memory is used alone; it also stimulates more insights into your character's thoughts.

There is another form of emotional memory that I want to bring to your attention. Call it an *imagined* emotional memory.

I first came across the need for this kind of experience when I was coaching Barbra Streisand for the Broadway production of *Funny Girl.*

It was our fifth weeek in Boston. My notes for Barbra's performance were getting more and more finicky—the larger, longer arcs of her character were mostly in place. But an emotional density was missing. Barbra's responses in the role were fine and varied, yet with many of her feelings, she would move into them then dismiss them too easily. Though we had worked on a multitude of different sensory and emotional memory choices, her feelings were not attaining a "critical mass."

One night, after an especially exhausting day of rehearsal and an evening performance, we retired to Barbara's hotel suite for my note-giving. Her energies were clearly spent. So I decided to forego my notes, and instead suggested that she treat herself to a well-deserved snack, then head off to bed.

We chatted on about various aspects of the show until room service arrived. Barbra set herself up on the sofa to munch away at her food. When she was fully involved in eating, I gently swung the conversation to more personal matters. I particularly wished to know if Barbra wanted her mother to be at the New York opening of the show. (In those days, her mother's presence led to tension and stress for Barbra).

Barbra wanted to know why I was asking that now. I said I was curious, because she so seldom talked about her family, yet obviously their relationships were important to her. She became more defensive; I asked her to lean back and breathe deeply. She wanted to resist, but began to follow my instructions. I talked her through a relaxation exercise, and in a few minutes, she was stretched out on the sofa, her head sunken deep into the cushion, looking very young and fragile.

I asked her again about inviting her mother to the New York

opening. She maintained the relaxation and answered with honesty. I asked her about inviting her sister and brother as well; she responded warmly and openly. Then I asked her about her father, who had died when she was still a small child.

Barbra almost bolted off the sofa. I had her refocus on relaxing, and assured her that she would be all right.

"Would you have wanted your father to be at that opening?" I asked her. "You know you've dreamt of it, of what your father would have been like. What your life would have been like if he were alive and here to see you and appreciate you. What he'd look like, and smell like, and feel like."

She started crying.

I said, "Keep imagining him—everything and anything you've ever thought about him. While you're doing that, pick the one song in the show you'd most want to sing for him."

The tears flowed even harder.

"Now cry, do whatever your feelings tell you, but don't let yourself tense up anywhere. Sing that song for your father, right here in this room."

It was a tremendous effort, but she did it. The song was glorious, and when she finished, she beamed with a sense of accomplishment.

I took her hands and told her how marvelous and moving she'd been. "Tomorrow night, I want you to imagine your father out there in the audience, and I want you to dedicate your entire performance to him. Will you do that?"

Her voice was quiet, almost broken by sobs again, but she firmly replied, "I'll try."

Barbra's performance the next night was the most emotionally charged one she had given. Every scene, every sequence, seemed to have gained an added dimension of vulnerability and caring.

I didn't take a single note that night.

I have used the technique of an imagined emotional memory countless times since. It can be practiced as an exercise.

Sit or lie down. Relax and pick a place—from at least five years ago. A place in which it was easy to be alone even if other people were around you, like a park, a beach, or a playground. Mull over all the sensory details of the place. Don't stick to any one time in the place; let your memory wander to different times.

When you are well-involved in the place, choose someone you haven't seen in a long time, someone who used to care about you a lot.

Try to imagine what that person would look like, abd be like, standing right behind you as you are sitting or lying down.

Pick the first song that pops into your head when you think of the person behind you, and without turning around, sing the song for that person.

And watch your emotions flow.

Then try out your monologue, or some dialogue from a scene, using that imaginary person as a judge of how honest and open you're being as you relate those words.

After you have practiced using different places, persons, and songs over a period of time, you'll find that some of them will remind you of specific emotional memory incidents that really happened. Let them move you where they will, and use whichever technique becomes the most appropriate.

How do you behave creatively in rehearsal or performance when, despite your best intentions, your emotions do not seem available?

A great actress of this century, Kim Stanley, was appearing in the Broadway production of William Inge's *Bus Stop*. Kim had already proven herself an actress of awesome character and emotional range. She was not usually at a loss for the appropriate feelings for her roles. But in an interview, she admitted that during a performance of the play, in a sequence where tears had always come from a certain experience she was using, she suddenly ran dry. Instead of panicking, she remembered what a teacher of hers had told her about using emotional memories: sometimes the performer will begin to take an event for granted, and not go through all the sensory details necessary to trigger the feelings.

So she paused, on stage, and quickly rethought the incident she'd been using, redefined the key sensory details in it, and almost immediately (perhaps ten seconds had elapsed) cried harder than she had in weeks. Without anyone on stage or in the audience even realizing she had almost gone dry.

Taking your task, or yourself, for granted is an easy path out of creative work. It can only dull you and conventionalize you.

Here's another alternative to use when the emotions won't flow. Psychiatrists have researched what many parents have known for centuries: Infants only two to three weeks old can mimic expressions on adult faces. Children twelve to eighteen months old, in the presence of their mothers, were given scary toys. Instead of immediately trying out these toys, most children checked their mother's faces for guidance. If the mother smiled serenely, the child went ahead and played. When the mother grimaced or showed fear, most children backed away, and some cried. Not a word had to be spoken. Children learn ways of seeing the world from adults' facial expressions. Later, as adults, the children (and the adults we grow up to be) still tend to connect facial expressions to feelings.

An experimental psychologist demonstrated by the use of objective physical measuring devices that people who assume certain facial expressions, especially those of anger, depression, fear, or sadness, actually feel corresponding inner sensations and physiological changes.

In other words, if you make the face of various feelings and lend yourself to their expression, you can trigger the feelings themselves.

Another way of putting this idea into practice is to behave as if you had certain feelings even if you don't. We all know that we sometimes don't feel lovingly toward our parents, but we are still capable of hugging and kissing them. We certainly are not always glad to see someone we call a friend, yet we effortlessly clasp their hands and smile in greeting. *Behave as if feelings were true and you will encourage those feelings to arise.*

But my favorite alternative for functioning creatively if your emotions are unavailable is illustrated by the following incident.

In the late 1950s, we had very special guests with us at the Actors Studio. The famed Kabuki Theater of Japan was performing a limited engagement on Broadway, their first visit since World War II, and their three biggest stars, all gentlemen in at least their mid-forties, had been invited to be with us.

Because Kabuki was so distant and stylized a theater company, most of us at the Studio, along with hundreds of fellow actors, had hurried to see the three plays done by them, which were fascinating. The Kabuki traditions were alienating to most of us: characters did not engage in person-to-person relationships, choruses would often tell the audience what was happening between the characters, and there was much singing of lines without emotional expression. But the performances were highly theatrical, the actors gorgeously costumed, and there were extravagant ensemble sequences of dance and mime.

In performance, one of the three guest artists far surpassed our expectations. I won't recount the plot, but only the substance of the sequence that startled all of us. During a disemboweling (hara-kiri) scene on stage, this actor cried actual tears. Not stylized sounds of emotion, but the real thing—tears streaming down his face, just like in our naturalistic theater and films.

This was unheard-of in Kabuki, so many of us in the Studio that day were there hoping for some enlightenment. Soon after the actors were introduced to us through their interpreter (they spoke no English), they suggested that rather than speak, we ask them questions, which most of us were eager to do. Anne Bancroft beat most of us to the main question on our minds. After some preliminary banter between Anne and the three gentlemen, she got to it hesitantly, not knowing whether the actor she addressed would quite understand.

"In that disemboweling scene you do"—he was instantly alert, smiled, and looked over at his interpreter—"you know, the hara-kiri scene?" He smiled even more generously and nodded. "I've seen it, and friends of mine have seen it at different times, and we've all noticed that you cry real tears."

The interpreter kept the actor very close to Anne's words, and he went on nodding. Anne gathered her courage and said, "Are you supposed to cry like that? I mean, are you allowed to? Nobody else in Kabuki does."

A quick consultation with his interpreter and the actor replied, "I don't know if I'm supposed to or not. Sometimes it just happens. Why?"

Anne held her tongue for a moment. Strasberg, a smiling

observer to their exchange, seemed to know what she really had in mind, and he prodded, "Go on, darling, ask him what you want—he'll tell you." The actor was delighted to be the cause of this high-level of interest. He looked from Lee to Anne, and in his own quick words and gestures, he encouraged her to speak further.

"Okay," Anne said, "when it does happen, you know, when you do cry, do you like it? I mean, do you want to cry? And if you do, *what do you use to get yourself to do it?*"

We all waited eagerly through the interpreting. The actor's eyes and face mirrored his pleasure at being asked these details of his technique. With great relish he spun out a question of his own. He was aware, said the interpreter, of some of Anne's acting, in films, and he had seen her cry many times. What did she use? His finger pointed right at her, and he gazed at her mischievously.

Again, Anne faltered slightly. I'm sure most of us knew why: it seemed ridiculous to tell an actor of this man's stature, coming from such a different cultural and theatrical background, the kinds of simple, personal acting images and devices we had all learned to use. Lee goaded her onward—"Go on, darling, tell him."

"Well," she said, with the actor demanding immediate translation from his interpreter, "sometimes I use certain words that open up painful memories, like trapped or failure." He nodded hard and made affirmative sounds. "Or sometimes I'll try to think of a difficult situation with my mother or father"—he kept nodding—"or someone else close to me."

He suddenly burst into an agreeing series of words and sounds (the interpreter flew to keep up with him). He then leaned forward with a half-helpless look on his face, and made movements with his fingers against his leg, accompanied by sounds that clearly illustrated pinching himself. He extended the movements and sounds, lifting his arms in an apologetic gesture that needed no interpretation. He was saying to us Americans—we primarily internally-oriented actors—that like all actors everywhere in the world, if we have to cry and can't figure out any other way to do it, we have to pinch ourselves.

The room exploded in appreciative laughter, and the actor

beamed at how shareable his example was. Those of us who were members of the Studio alternately laughed and tossed words at each other: "Incredible," "Just like us," "I don't believe it."

Anne, who had joined in the response as much as anyone else, was persistent. She calmed us all down, then with full confidence and warm tone, she responded, "Okay. Me, too. All of us, too. But what I really want to know is, if you do cry, when you *do* cry during that scene, what usually makes that happen?"

The actor nodded gently, thoughtfully, and an expectant silence came over the room. "In my country," he said, "I usually cry when I hear people in the audience do so. I am very moved that I have moved them. Sometimes as I carry out the ritual of hara-kiri, it stirs feelings that make me cry. The only thing I know to do is carry out this ritual as beautifully as I can. What then happens, I cannot foretell."

Everyone in the room nodded. The truth and incisiveness of his answer was inescapable. We were all moved. It was the reply of an artist at the height of his powers sharing with us a self-evident, utterly simple, but too-often-forgotten acting truism: carry out your choice "as beautifully as you can," and what results is not your concern—it will have its own life, especially in the theater, where every blending of audience and actors creates another mixture. The shape and structure of a performance will never move any one audience precisely the way it moves another.

While no one can guarantee absolute results in acting, I have never found a more consistent avenue to emotional responses and character behavior than through the use of sense and emotional memories. Every one of us contains an ocean of responses and behaviors to draw upon. Or we can use the same choices over and over and still achieve infinite variety by changing combinations. When you discover that you possess this enormous capacity for expression and have the means to channel this expressiveness into a wide variety of roles, you'll come as close as actors ever get to nirvana.

Shangri-La for most mortals means a place of utter peace and contentment. For actors, it is that location within, the place where we test the limits of our emotions, and from which all human behavior eventually flows.

Finding Your Self

A unique and sometimes powerful exercise-improvisation called the *private moment* was developed by Lee Strasberg to help actors, professional or beginning, unlock a special inhibition, which at least temporarily allowed the actor to use himself more unconventionally.

A private moment is a sequence of activity—either physical, mental, or both—that the individual would stop or do differently if any other person were present. It doesn't have to be momentous. It can be simply facing yourself in the mirror as you shave or put on makeup, while admitting thoughts and feelings about yourself. It could be writing in your diary. It could be the way you eat when you know you're not being watched.

On the bulletin board in the reception area at the Actors Studio each session's participants were usually listed a week or two in advance. Some members would then decide, based on who was working that day, whether to attend or not. One morning, Shelley Winter's name appeared on the advance list, and alongside it was the description "a private moment."

Shelley, by this time, was more famous than the exercise. She was not only a star on stage and in films, she was rather singularly known as one of the least inhibited performers in New York or Hollywood. Why was she bothering with this particular exercise? Many of us discussed the possible reasons, none of us were sure, so on the day of Shelley's scheduled exercise, the Studio was packed.

What she did seemed too simple. There were no explosions, no bursts of emotion or temperament. It was a quiet improvisation about getting ready for sleep, with just a touch of tearful contemplation in a mirror, and a very palpable but peaceful sense of aloneness. It lasted twenty minutes or so.

When it was over, Shelley, looking doe-eyed and vulnerable, glanced around the room seeking signs of recognition and approval from her many friends and peers in the room. Her audience, including me, was silent. No one seemed moved by or taken with the exercise. We were perplexed by what it was all for, and no one spoke for a long time—until Strasberg said, "Darling, tell everybody why you did this."

Now a little unsure of herself, Shelley described a conversation with Lee in which she admitted a deep concern she had had for a long time about her emotional life in various roles she'd played. She spoke quietly, steadily, as she named some of the roles, and then a sudden deep sobbing voice emerged as she expressed her anguish at repeating the same emotional pattern over and over regardless of the differences in her characters. "I always cry the same. I'm always a victim," she wailed, "and I hate it, but I can't seem to keep myself from doing it!"

Immediately, we all recognized Shelley's need to try this private moment, and all our doubts and negative responses seemed ridiculous and narrow-minded. Some of us applauded her, some of us called out our appreciation, and almost all of us came away from that session with a much deeper appreciation of the value of challenging and sometimes changing our emotional habits.

Even before Shelley's effort, I had admired other actors' breakthrough experiences using a private moment. So I had searched for one I could bring in, but without success. I seemed unable to discover or admit something I did that was so private I would have to change or stop it in anyone else's presence.

But one day I did. I realized that I danced to all kinds of music only when no one was around. I did it rarely, maybe twice a year, but whenever I did do it, I always felt extremely private and vulnerable. I never danced socially.

With great anticipation I signed up for my exercise. Three days before I was scheduled, the fear factor set in. I hardly slept. I was anxious even among friends and family. I told no one what I was going to do.

The day arrived only too soon. I was second on the schedule. I didn't watch the scene done before me, nor did I listen to any comments. I only waited. And sweated. I felt that this morning could be crucial to my acting life.

As I finished the exercise, I was certain I'd done something important. My entire body told me so. I was full of excited sensations and throbbing all through me. When I looked out at the audience, I was dumbfounded: most of the actors in the room were looking elsewhere. Lee himself sighed deeply, and also looked away. Except for a few close friends, not one person seemed interested.

I waited. All the heat in my body seemed to evaporate. And I suddenly felt trepidation. They all looked as though I'd done something wrong.

Finally, speaking slowly, Lee addressed me: "This was a private moment?"

I couldn't answer.

"This is something you would stop doing if someone else came into the room?"

"Yes, yes." Though my body was cool, my response was heated.

"All right," he said.

"I don't understand," I said.

"Neither do I," he replied. "Do you always do it just this way? Is this the music you always use? Is this the way you dress when you do it? Do you ever do it in your underwear, or naked?"

"No, never." I was so outraged at his questions that several people laughed. "Sometimes it's this music, sometimes it's different. Everything else is just the way I dance when I'm alone. I even set the time of day so I'd know I'd be alone."

"All right, all right," Lee said. "It's not that I disbelieve you. What you did"—he hesitated, then continued—"seemed"—he was having difficulty defining what he thought, and I hung desperately on his every word—"well, it was personal, yes. I believe that. But somehow it just didn't feel private. It just didn't."

I stared, incredulous. He turned to the room.

"Anybody else feel differently?"

Many heads nodded no.

I stared at everyone, the awful feeling of failure within me.

His tone changed. He suddenly sounded compassionate.

"I don't know why, Allan. As you describe it, it should have been a private moment, but it wasn't. Don't give up on it. Take it home and think it over again. See if maybe there was some ingredient you left out."

And that was it. Friends comforted me, a few others smiled apologetically. It was a total letdown.

It took another two days of mulling the event over for the revelation to hit.

I called the Studio office to reschedule myself as soon as there was an opening. I even asked to be called if there was a last-minute cancellation. A week later there was. I wasn't anxious this time; I was excited. I felt really adventurous, and most of all curious.

There wasn't much of a crowd that day. And I was first. I was dressed exactly the same as I'd been last time, with exactly the same music, and I began the exercise. Only this time I didn't dance the way I always had—I danced the way *I wished I could dance*. I went up into the balcony and leaped off like Gene Kelly might. I tap-danced around a column holding up the balcony as Fred Astaire might if the column was an imaginary partner. I did dance steps I didn't know I could do.

When the record finished this time my body wasn't throbbing, it felt cleansed. My feelings were joyous, I felt as if I had triumphed over something impossible for me. And when I looked at Lee and my fellow actors, they were beaming and nodding: yes.

Lee immediately asked me what I had done differently. "Everything," I replied. "I've never danced like that in my entire life. Even in my private life, I've never allowed myself to be *that private*."

Back in the days when I was studying with Uta Hagen, she once confided to us that the real reason she felt she failed in her opening scene of the Broadway production of *Saint Joan* was because she was so busy playing who she was, where she had come from, who she was going to see and why, that she forgot to act the scene. We all laughed (and so did she, since it was many months after the show had closed), but later I began to wonder how that was possible. If you had prepared yourself with all those details of character, text, and action, how was it possible not to play the scene?

I believe, in retrospect, another reason was the key factor: Uta, in life, was a strapping woman, handsome as all get-out but very peasant-like in her physical behavior. Mentally, socially, political-ly, she was adroit and knowledgeable, but her actual physical movements were simple and rather lumbering. I think she had an idea in her head that because of her mental prowess and attrac-tive persona she had to convince her audience right from the beginning of the play that she could act a peasant girl (Joan). So she spent much of her energy displaying those qualities, rather than focusing on the playing of the scene.

Shelley's predisposition toward one kind of crying, my inability to admit my inhibitions even to myself, and Uta's concern with her own physicality were manifestations of what I call habits.

Most of us carry around a good deal of habits, some in the form of mental or emotional attitudes, some of them physical. The outwardly physical kinds are the easiest to spot—and clearly the easiest to change. Take the case of an athlete. A good baseball batter goes into a slump but doesn't know why; the coaches pool their observations and recommend a change of batting stance or timing. A dancer's pirouette loses its grace; the dance master or choreographer reworks the dancer's lead-in movements and more practice sessions are scheduled.

But how do you stop a chocolate junkie's physical depen-dence? Or a Coca-Cola addict's? Or an alcoholic's or drug abuser's? Psychological and emotional habits are often even tougher to deal with. (How many times have you tried to con-vince a friend that he or she keeps making the same mistake in a choice of lover?)

Too many competent, accomplished human beings, seemingly at the threshold of major developments in their careers, begin to fail or fade, or repeat past successes rather than adventure for-ward. So many human beings in all walks of life, with the capaci-ties to fulfill myriad accomplishments, never seem to rise to the level of their possibilities. Organizations and programs such as EST and Scientology, self-help books and counselors, therapists, and religious leaders all gain multitudes of followers by promising to eradicate doubts and nonproductive habits, to release one's well-being and productive energies.

It seems self-evident to me that for most people, almost every day of one's waking life is ninety-five to ninety-nine percent habitual. No one I know ever walks into a bakery shop and behaves the way he or she truly feels; the cookies would all be eaten in minutes. If everyone waiting in a dentist's office were to admit what was actually going on inside them, the moanings and groanings would make that waiting room sound like the first portal of hell.

Even the language we use to communicate our feelings tends to be habitual: "I was really angry." "I went a little crazy." "She made me so happy." "What a great view."

When an entire theater or movie audience is suddenly prone to coughing just before the performance begins (or at dull sequences during the performance), is it because a cloud of dust has been let loose in the auditorium? Or is it an opportunity for patrons to cover up their complaints ("I paid enough for these tickets, it better be worth it," or "That woman's hairdo is blocking my view," or "This play stinks, what was that reviewer talking about?") without interrupting the actors or those around them? The coughing is a group habit, socially acceptable and yet quite private, since no one ever actually knows what someone else may be coughing about at that moment.

Or take scratching. If you were to print time-lapse photos of all your scratchings during the course of a single day, you wouldn't believe how many there were. You would seem never to stop. There isn't a person alive who doesn't scratch himself somewhere almost continually every day. (Certain cultures avoid this by using worry beads—people stroke the beads instead of their bodies.) Surely these perpetual itches cannot be caused by constant invisible droppings of cobwebs. Certain phrases have entered our vocabulary to explain what is actually going on: "I was itching to do it" or "the seven-year itch." These are inner itches, inner sensations that we express in disguise.

Our bodies tingle continuously with sensations that are actually caused by feelings or impulses that for one reason or another we suppress. The energies triggered by these impulses must go some-where. The quickest, safest social outlet for them is coughing, clearing our throats, scratching, or shifting our body positions. We cough or scratch or shift the undesired impulse away, and no one is the wiser. Unfortunately, that usually includes ourselves, since we never seem to take the time and trouble to try to decipher these multitudinous signals from our inner recesses. And there we have another massive habit.

Obviously, some habits or customs are helpful. A periodic checkup at the doctor's or dentist's can be crucial to your health; sending remembrances for a birthday or anniversary maintains warm relationships; a period of mourning is essential in facing the death of a loved one.

But when habits or customs interfere with our work, or our relationships, or our creativity, those repetitive patterns must be replaced, or we will never attain full and gratifying use of our capacities.

One of my roles at a well-respected summer theater was the man in a two-character play, *Two for the Seesaw*. It was a wonderful role, complex and deep. The director was not only a friend, he was also my teaching partner at our studio in Manhattan. By the third day, my leading lady and I were really cooking along; we felt involved and adventurous, scenes were beginning to crackle, when all of a sudden the director, Curt Conway, stopped us and said he'd like to see me on the side for a minute.

The opportunity for a private tête-à-tête with a good director is always a little intimidating. I knew I must have done some-thing wrong. With trepidation, I jumped down off the stage. He put his arm around me and walked me out into the sunshine. Outside, he faced me and put his hands on my shoulders. His eyes were warm and encouraging as he said, "Allan, my friend and confrere, you are really wonderful in this part. You'd be even more wonderful if you'd laugh out loud once in a while." He paused. I stared. He realized I was confused. "I see you smile," he continued, "but you don't make any laughing *sounds*. So your pleasure doesn't really communicate to me in the audi-ence, and it leaves me a little cool about you. I should feel warm about you. So would you please change your smiles to laughs? With sound?"

I said, "Of course. It wasn't really deliberate. I'd be happy to put some laughter in my part."

What I didn't tell him was that in my personal life I never laughed out loud. As a kid, I lived in a home with an uncle who was ill for many years. I could never play or speak up loudly in the house, so I always ended up in our basement, alone or with friends, having to keep my laughing silent. And as an adult, I'd never heard any comments or complaints about my silent laughter.

What I was unprepared for was how difficult and awkward it would be in my adult life to finally produce sound to fill those silent smiles. I tried to laugh like most people do, you know, in keeping with the circumstances. That wasn't good enough, for almost nothing came out. My laughing pipes were too rusted, or encrusted. So I had to laugh four times louder than anyone around me. At company meals, in rehearsals, backstage, whenever someone said anything remotely funny, I cranked out what passed for laughing. It was horrible. It was devastating. For three full days I pursued a recognizable and acceptable sound of laughter, till just before the first performance, when Curt put his arm around me and said the equivalent of "By God, he's done it!"

I've used the word "habit" to cover a variety of behaviors very deliberately, because to me a habit, unlike a problem, has been learned. Once identified, it can be unlearned, or bent, or broken, or replaced by a new, better habit, whereas a problem has to be solved (and heaven help you if you don't solve it).

Early in my membership at the Actors Studio, Strasberg was rather fond of me as an actor. He would smile regularly at me after a scene I had done—half-appreciatively, half-skeptically—and he would say things like, "That was very good, Allan. I don't know if I believed you or not. Do another scene." I tended to take those remarks as compliments: Pretty terrific to be able to fool the old man like that, he couldn't tell if I was really into it or not. Young ego at work.

Gradually, over a period of a year, his seeming admiration turned to harsher criticisms. My work was getting sloppy. Self-indulgent. Unimaginative.

So I worked harder, relying less on my intuitions and imitations and more on craft. I also took all the extra, special classes given free at the Studio—mime, T'ai-chi-chuan, fencing, sense and emotional memory. I became a regular observer, at Lee's invitation, of his private classes, and other classes about town as well.

I kept what became a voluminous notebook on different techniques applied to hundreds of individual actors in all these classes—what worked, and for whom, and what didn't. I read all the books by Stanislavski, Boleslavsky, Michael Chekhov, Robert Lewis, Harold Clurman, and many others.

I began to comment more on other actors' work (that was encouraged at the Studio). My criticisms became valued. Actors asked me to coach them as favors. Lee recommended me, and I was hired, to teach at a professional acting school.

My own acting work gained in execution. I was complimented regularly for its precision and its clarity. I felt stronger, more defined, as an actor.

But not creative. The more my skill flourished, the less acceptable my acting became. I was called cold, aloof, uninvolved. I became very depressed and left the Studio.

I continued to teach and work Off-Broadway and on television. I began writing scripts and sold four to the Canadian Broadcasting Corporation. Away from the Studio, I actually functioned surprisingly well on acting jobs. I didn't feel dispassionate or unimaginative most of the time. My auditions were full-blooded, and my performances were more than decently received.

But some leftover alley-cat gene kept gnawing at me (or maybe it was the residual effect of being raised in Brooklyn). I was angry and disappointed to have left the Studio feeling like a semi-failure, so after many months away, I decided to return and try again, by effort and observation, to see what I was somehow still missing.

A couple of scenes later, having worked as diligently as I could at my chosen material, Lee was still nodding his head negatively when it was time to appraise my efforts. However, at the end of my third return scene, in the midst of his criticism, he hesitated, and stopped. His critical tone changed, sounded warmer, more partner-like, as he addressed me.

"Allan, I'm not sure about this, but it seems to me that there are two of you operating up there when you act."

That statement caught me right by my root-hairs.

"One part of you seems to want to act the scene the very best you can, and you come in armed with really good sensory choices, actions, and character choices and whatever else you think you should be working on, but I don't know..."

I never heard Lee say the words "I don't know." I was quiet as he continued: "It seems to me—I feel like there's another part of you that just as strongly wants something else, but I don't know what."

Those magic words again, he didn't know. I was mesmerized.

"You've been teaching for a while now. If you know what I'm talking about, maybe you have some exercise or something you do in your class that would help. I'm not sure, but I think you know more about this than I do. Think about it and see if you can bring in something that could open this up. All right?"

I was very close to toppling off the edge of my chair. I nodded yes, while my brain began racing. The perception of what he was saying prodded me, but I couldn't quite hold the idea in focus. For days, I mulled over his observation incessantly. Besides trying to act the hell out of the part, what other force could there possibly be? In me or in any other actor? Did he mean something psychological, like a repressed Oedipal something? Or a desire to be immortal? Or just wanting to get good reviews? I mean, how potent could this thing be, and why did it have to function so negatively in me ?

Sleeping was not easy those next few days. One of my persistent thoughts became, If one part of me is so occupied with the need to act well, how could I ever find out what this other part might be? It seemed impossible.

Ahh, but desperation becomes the real mother of invention. I calculated that since the Acting-Well Force was dominant, the only way I might discover this other Hidden Force was to act unwell. Unprepared. No acting choices whatsoever. Nada.

This sounded crazy. But interesting. How would I go about acting something that had no preparation? The best I could come up with was this: Pick a part I could never be cast in, and choose a

scene but don't learn the lines. Then act out in sounds and movements whatever happened to me while I was out there unprepared in front of the class. Aiy-aiy-aiy. Just the idea of doing that
terrified me. But I was driven to try.

I found a television script by Rod Serling about a teenage
Puerto Rican delinquent named Dino. I chose a scene when he's
alone with a psychiatrist. I asked a fellow actor in the Studio, Ron
Leibman, to do this "thing" with me. (Ron was known for his willingness to try almost anything for acting purposes.) When I
explained what I had in mind, Ron asked, "If you're not going to
learn the lines, how will I know when to talk?"

"After I've made a few noises, I guess—you'll have to use your
own judgment."

"What the hell," he said, "that's what psychiatrists do anyway."

We were on the bill two weeks later. We had one pseudo-
rehearsal to try out the idea. Ron would say a line, I'd push out
some kind of noise at him, and he would continue. I'd had to
read over the scene once just to see if it was suitable, and every
so often, in between my noises, a phrase sounding like a line in
the script would pop into my head, and since part of my task was
to express anything that happened to me while I was working, I
would say those words. But my main focus was to search out the
Secret Force.

I didn't find it in that rehearsal. I didn't find very much of anything else, either—no big emotions, no enlightened behavior. Ron
asked if I really wanted to do it at the Studio. I felt no, but I said
yes.

Three days before we were scheduled my body went into a
tailspin. Nothing functioned without tension and pain. I lost my
appetite, I barely slept, my temperature seemed to fluctuate
between polar and tropical degrees. I didn't convulse, but I did
think I might implode. I isolated myself from my family, trying to
get a grip on myself. I felt like I should get a doctor's note to
keep me from going to class.

The day arrived. Ron stayed with me off on the side while the
class assembled. I sweated and palpitated until it was time. Lee
announced our exercise/scene. Ron walked out to take his place
at a desk he had set up. I didn't think I could move; my legs were

weighted. From deep within me, a kind of howl suddenly emerged, my hands locked on either side of my head, and I forcibly dragged myself in front of the group. I had placed a single chair in front of the desk. I marched toward it, my eyes focused only on the floor, until I reached it. I was still howling. I looked up at Ron. He had lit a cigarette and was watching me, coolly but observantly. Another sound arose in me, a growl. I sat in the chair staring at him, and my body began to rock, slowly, rhythmically. He spoke. I rocked and started singing under my breath—not a song, just a kind of rocking-soothing-singing. Ron said his next line, and so it went for several minutes, until a very strange impulse struck me. It seemed so unlikely that I resisted it. I forgot all about my task, and why I was doing this damn exercise. I got really hot. My body contorted, my arms and legs seemed to disconnect from me, but my head held firm. It actually felt rigid. My eyes lost focus. And then came The Force—a wave, a wall of...something...demanding my attention. Some fearful noise emanated from within me as I turned my head, eyes stuck and staring, from Ron to the audience of actors. I couldn't believe I was doing it. It was against every principle and attitude of acting I'd been trained to. No fourth wall. No making believe they weren't there. No concentration on what I was acting. I just had to see if anybody cared or if they had all left the room.

I saw them all, including Lee and his wife Paula, riveted on me. Mostly expressionless, but riveted. They seemed poised for something to happen. I looked from person to person and they stared back. I turned to Ron and he was staring now just as intently. I looked at the audience again. They were so engrossed by what I was doing that tears began to well up in me; I felt so grateful for their interest. When I cried, they cried—Paula too, even Lee. I was dumbfounded, and started laughing in relief. When I laughed, they laughed—everybody in the room, it seemed. I turned again to Ron, and there he was, laughing just as much as anyone, but wiping his eyes as well.

I couldn't understand what was happening, my emotions were so mixed. Ron continued with some dialogue. I mostly made sounds. The Force returned. I had to look out at the class again. With awful feelings of apology I turned to see what had become of everyone; there they were, right with me, smiles of approval, tears of recognition. Paula waved and smiled at me like one of those loving aunts at a family gathering, letting me know I was all right, a valued member of the family.

My feelings were deeper than I knew what to do with. I was wounded but happy, grateful yet confused. I turned back to Ron again, both of us now catapulting our words and sounds toward one another to finish off the scene.

We soon did. I sat limply, more used, more vulnerable, than I could remember. Lee was extremely patient, giving both Ron and me ample time to speak about what we had tried to do. Lee complimented Ron on his work and on his responsiveness, then turned to me.

"Do you know what you did, Allan? Do you know what you accomplished?"

All I could do was gape.

"First of all," he said, "I've got to tell you that I've never seen a better demonstration of something all actors feel, the biggest fear of all, the fear of looking foolish in front of an audience. By coming in unprepared, you laid yourself bare to this fear, and I think—I believe—this is that other Force I was talking about. You have it in spades. But you're not alone, you just expressed more of it than most actors would be willing to admit. Also, by expressing everything you could about its effects on you, you released something else: inspiration."

Tangling with a concept always excited him. Paula and others were hanging on his words. I still just felt limp.

"Do you have any idea what you did *for the scene?*"

That snapped my brain to attention.

"I wasn't trying to do the scene," I said.

"Exactly." Everyone laughed, including me. I felt silly.

"By removing your usual preparations, you allowed other facets of your experience and intuition to operate. You got your conscious brain out of the way so your real perceptions of the material could function."

"What perceptions?" I asked. "I only read the damn thing once. I didn't have any perceptions."

"You don't think you did, but you did. You read the material, you knew what was in it, that's how you decided that you couldn't possibly do it. Okay, so you're not a Puerto Rican delinquent; you may not have ever even been a delinquent [everyone laughed] and I wasn't there when you were growing up. The point is, somewhere inside you was an understanding of what that fifteen-year-old was going through."

My mouth was hanging open, my mind jumping to comprehend what he meant.

"Do you remember," he went on, "when you were hanging off the edge of the chair watching the smoke from Ron's cigarette spread into the air?"

"Absolutely."

"Could you tell us what you were thinking then?"

"Sure." It was crystal clear in my memory. But suddenly the words seemed difficult. "I was thinking of my brother..." I stopped.

"Yes?"

"He was younger than me..."

"It's all right, go ahead." He was extremely gentle and I was very touched.

"We'd shared a room—even the same bed—most of our lives, till I was about seventeen, when I went into the Army...." Tears welled up in my eyes and my throat constricted.

"Go ahead, we'll wait."

Not wanting to take up everybody's time, I pushed through. "So when I was watching the smoke, I noticed it came off the cigarette in one stream, but then it started to split up"—I couldn't stop the crying then, and it burst out—"just like my brother and me." I was crying and talking at the same time. "Whenever he got into trouble at school, or with my mother or my father, I used to take care of him. A lot. But then we started to split up, dissolve, just like that smoke!"

I was gone, I couldn't talk. The emotions felt deeper and more painful than during the scene. I couldn't even look at anyone.

Lee spoke again. "Do you know what line of dialogue you said at that time?"

My head came up and the tears retreated. "I didn't say anything, did I? I just made noises."

"Oh, you made plenty of those," he said. Another big warm laugh surrounded me. He looked at one of the index cards he always made notes on during a scene. "But you also said 'Nobody at home understands me, nobody.' Is that a line from the script?"

Ron jumped in, "It sure is. It's one of the few cues he gave me." We all laughed.

Lee had four more quotes for me. All close to dialogue in the script, all rendered during excruciating emotional and physical sequences of behavior, all expressive of the situation in the script. I hardly remembered saying the few lines, I'd been so intent on expressing what was happening to me. He pointed out that those lines written by the author helped me express what I was thinking and feeling, that's why I used them instead of sounds.

The whole event made me recognize that all of us, from even the first reading of a script, have already ingested pertinent emotional and psychological information about the characters, the situation, and the plot. It's all there for us to use, but our emotional and psychological habits tend to make us suppress these connections if we believe they'll be unpleasant or painful.

We all understand what an exorcism is meant to be: entering into experiences that seem darkly terrifying to clear them from our systems. That's what I was able to accomplish that day at the Studio. Instead of trying to arrange myself in relation to the material so that I could act it safely, I removed the conscious, acceptable, habitual part of me—the fearful part—and *allowed everything that touched my emotions for the role to flow out of me*. It was a great captive state to be in. I wished I'd discovered this process years earlier.

In the late 1960s, Jerzy Grotowski created a theater in Poland that for years became the capstone for inspirational acting in the Western world. He called it "poor theater," meaning it had no reliance on lighting tricks, ingenious set designs, or other production elements, but was based only on the actors' illuminations of the text. All impulses were to stem directly from the actors. There was to be no choreography or direction in the usual sense; the director was there merely as an editor, to sift out the most insightful expressions and behavior that arose in rehearsal. To accomplish this feat, Grotowski selected a small band of actors, moved them to the countryside away from all urban distractions, and there began a two-year disciplinary training program, the central purpose of which was "to scourge them of all social habits."

In the early 1930s, another famous acting company called The Group Theatre found its best ways of working away from their urban background. They, too, trained themselves off in the countryside, where their usual individual habits and patterns of life would not keep them from the new forms of acting they were seeking.

Artists and non-artists alike have recognized this truth for centuries: if it is true that ninety-odd percent of every day and night we are walking, talking, behaving creatures of habit, then how is it possible for any of us to automatically be able to be open, fresh, and original for whatever the task or material we wish to work at? It's impossible—unless we find a process that moves us from our habitual frame of mind, we will react just as habitually to a script as we do to everything else around us.

The single most controversial and complex habit we all have to deal with concerns our concept of who we are.

When a person asks "How are you?," which "you" replies? If a friend is concerned and wants to know "What's going on with you?," which "you" answers?

Soon after my episode with The Force at the Studio, I started trying to define the possible differences between my habitual self and my unexposed, truest self. I had read many cases of psychiatric treatments that helped uncover patients' hidden selves. I knew of individuals finding truths within through religious beliefs. I had alcoholic friends who found release for their inner beings by banding with others in group confrontations or by going cold turkey, facing their internal demons alone.

None of these processes seemed to be what I was looking for. I wanted a simple, easily applicable procedure that anyone could apply at any time and get reasonably close to an unhabitual frame of mind.

One night I was up late, my family already asleep, and I was struggling restlessly for an answer. I turned on the radio quietly, just to listen to some music and rest my thoughts. I lay down on the living room sofa and let myself hum along with whatever was playing. It was the Boston Pops Orchestra's recording of some popular tunes. The third song played was "You And The Night And The Music," a big hit in those days. I began singing the words, "You, and the night, and the music/Fill me with thoughts so divine..." The incisiveness of that phrase struck me. I repeated it. I stopped singing and began going over the lyrics. I turned off the radio. It seemed clear that to engender "thoughts so divine" (who wouldn't want to have some thoughts like that?) I'd have to be available to the night and the music—and the "you" in that song had to be the realest, truest person possible. The "night" was whatever was around me; the "music" had to be something that moved me. Here it was—a combination that confirmed what I'd been thinking about, a combination I could clearly follow and explore.

I remembered that like everyone else I knew, every once in a while, usually due to a build-up of stressful involvements or actions, I needed to be by myself. Needed to remove my regular self from everyday entanglements in order to see where *I* was really at. And that usually involved a long walk somewhere, or several hours or days at the ocean or a retreat, or, at the very least, staying home without answering the phone or the doorbell. Sometimes such a crisis made me need the presence of a friend or loved one, but if I made an invitation, it was just to be together, without distractions, trying to get all kinds of thoughts and feelings to pour out of me. Now how to get in touch with this evasive and complex sense of myself (so I could see it in others) without actually going away or calling in friends? I had to think myself over a little. How little? How much?

I arbitrarily chose a week. I challenged myself to mull over the past week of my life and try to discern "who" I had been most of that time. Did I dress any differently than usual? Even for a gathering or to go play softball? Did I try any very different foods? When I spoke to friends or family, did I tend to cover the usual subjects with them? When I met or became involved with strangers, was I my typically surfacey self?

Was there any opportunity to be truer than my habitual self, and if so, had I taken it? Why not? If this past week had been my last on this earth, would I want to have been remembered for it?

Though many of my feelings were upsetting, as an actor I was exhilarated by the flood of emotions and thoughts these questions raised in me. The process of reviewing just one recent week in my life seemed a remarkably short and unperilous path to vulnerability. I felt as though I was revealing much of my realer self.

If I could maintain this unique sense of myself by these questions and observations of my past week's behavior, then be open to whatever was around me, I would have achieved the first two parts of that lyric "*You* and *the night...*" All I needed then was to choose appropriate "music" and the equation would be complete, and I might arrive at "thoughts so divine." This was just as tricky as trying to find that other Force that Lee had put me on to, but it was also wonderfully involving.

Suppose I try various pieces of music, I thought, and see what happens? Good idea. I closed my eyes to rethink much of my previous week, until I was clearly in touch with my patterns and habits again. And my missed opportunities. As feelings arose in me—and they did—I began to make sounds from within myself, and again felt in touch with a truer me. I then opened my eyes to include the room and the details of life around me (which was "the night"), and I began to hum the first piece of music that popped into my head. It was the first movement from Beethoven's Third Symphony, the *Eroica*.

As deep as my feelings had been up to this point, the music stirred subterranean caverns in my being. Long looping swells of emotion seemed to wash through me: sad, triumphant, romantic. Though I am not much of a singer, I sang heroically for a long time that day. Tears of pleasure, sometimes pain, arose, along with wonderfully emotional images of family and friends, current and past. Stories I had read from long ago flashed through me, feelings rising in continual surges, full and passionate. And I continued to sing. In a voice barely known to me, I sang the *Eroica* theme and other parts of the symphony, using every part of my voice I could get to. I felt I could go on for hours. I was feeling really "divine."

To further test what I had done, after some time (I don't know how long, it could have been five minutes or twenty), I decided to change the music. To see how a different combination would change my feelings.

I closed my eyes and rethought the circumstances of my previous week (which seemed to come quickly now). I relaxed myself into the feelings that again began to stir. When I felt involved, I tried to open myself to everything around me, and then was about to pick another piece of music when unexpectedly, the words of a Robert Frost poem, "Stopping by Woods on a Snowy Evening," popped into my head. The simple but pointed thoughts expressed in the poem suddenly seemed revelatory to me, and beautiful. I recited as many of the words as I could recall, and felt myself totally—physically, emotionally, psychologically, philosophically—in harmony with the poem. I spoke the lines several times over and they never dimmed. I felt open, released, fluid. Kind of "divine" again.

And all of a sudden, I found myself drawn to a speech I'd been working on for a play I was to do. The words hurried into my mind. I rattled them off with great energy and strangely connected feelings. After one time through I repeated the words, only this time I whispered them and went very slowly. The energy was still there but muted, controlled. The feelings intensified. I wanted a third try: this time I sang the words using a made-up melody. The words gained again in celebration, and so did I. I seemed ready for and available to any possible interpretation of the speech—lyrical, satirical, silly, sentimental, patriotic. I could have gone on for hours rehearsing possibilities. I felt not only divine but inspired.

I've repeated this exercise using different speeches, poems, and lyrics many, many times. Every time I carried out the structure and involvement well—took the time necessary to reintroduce myself to the unhabitual "me," allowed the circumstances of place to surround me, then moved into the material I had chosen—I found insights, emotional connections, and a surprising range of interpretation available to me.

And of course I have used this "You And The Night And The Music" exercise in hundreds of classes and coaching assignments.

It has proven to be invaluable in helping isolate and define the "you" in most of us.

Here again, in a nutshell, is its basic form (innovations on it are welcome). First select a speech or a monologue that you're working on. Begin by closing your eyes, breathing deeply, relaxing, and mulling over your preceding week. Try to distinguish your familiar patterns of behavior in eating, dressing, activities, and relationships. Ask yourself if there were any opportunities to behave differently, other than your usual, habitual self. If this past week had been your last to be remembered by, what would you think of yourself?

When you feel involved with these thoughts and the feelings they arouse, continue your questioning and open your eyes to add in the "night," which is whatever is actually around you at that moment— the time, the place, objects, people (or lack of people). See what's there. If people are around you, look at each person, trying to be the truest "you" you can, allowing each person to look into your eyes for a glimpse of that realer "you."

After you are engaged with the "night," sing or hum the first piece of music that pops into your head, or have someone around you suggest one, and if it's familiar enough, use it. You may then shift to a second piece of music. Or a poem. Or the lyrics of a song. And then on to your chosen speech or monologue.

And bring this process with you into rehearsals. It's not just an exercise, it's a way to unleash the originalities in you. And hopefully, with a little practice, you will soon achieve some measure of "divinity" in your acting work.

Another major area of habitual difficulty for the actor is the concept of freedom. Whenever I have been asked to "do whatever I felt like" while rehearsing a scene or monologue, it's been almost impossible. Even with the encouragement to be as free as you can, most people, including actors, don't know how to do that. It's never been part of any adult's curriculum. With all our everyday, habitual, reserved ways of behaving heavy upon us, how do we suddenly become freewheeling instruments of instantly-accessible impulses? A little structure helps.

Instead of allowing any old impulse to take root at any time in any old way while you're doing a monologue or scene, select three movements before you begin: one for the arms, one for the legs, and one for somewhere else (the head, the torso, the butt), it doesn't matter where. I use the number three for the old Biblical and mythical reasons, but it could easily be four or five. Two has turned out to be too limiting.

Arbitrarily and irregularly (which means don't decide ahead of time which movement you'll use for which line), pump one of those movements into your body as you go through the speech. Don't just snap it in and out. Do each movement with force and conviction, but let it last a little while before you withdraw it. And don't feel like you have to do the movements in order. Repeat one several times if you wish, see what happens.

Invariably you'll find the movements, arbitrary though they seemed when you picked them, often have a validity you couldn't anticipate. They give expression where you hadn't thought of any. They keep you from illustrating the words with conventional gestures. And they keep you off-balance enough so that you don't restrain what you're actually feeling because you weren't sure those feelings were suitable. In other words, you have provided physical channels *for sensations, thoughts, and feelings that otherwise might have wandered away for lack of your knowing what to do with them.*

Even if one of the movements you choose turns out to be rather banal, next time around simply choose a more interesting one, or one you believe to be more in keeping with the character whose words you are striving to act. A choice of movement can be poor, and even wrong for the part. So what? It's only a movement, very easily changed. That's the whole point. Right or wrong, weak or inspired, it's definable, it's changeable, it's accessible. In the meantime, it gives your body behavioral assignments to behave, movements that can contain any thought or feeling of which you are capable.

There is no freedom without choices. Making a choice leaves you free to invent on it, around it, within it. You can make the worst choice possible, but if you carry it out well, *you're* okay. *You* functioned well. Next time you'll choose more appropriately.

Now I want to present you with a variation of this three-movement exercise-improvisation, one that enters a different but vital area.

Most of us have been conditioned (not trained) to presume that we will behave mostly in keeping with our feelings. We are expected to be reasonable enough to express pleasure when we're pleased, anger when we're disappointed or frustrated, and when we are unsure of what we feel, to pass over those feelings until we are clearer.

Let me suggest doing the opposite instead.

As you traffic with your monologue or scene, whenever you feel pleased with the way it's going, behave aggressively; hit things (not just with your hands, try a foot or your back), bounce on the furniture, raise your voice, even punch out. (Don't actually hit your partner, beat the air around him instead; once you have a director, you can work out any actual blows.)

When you seem to feel badly about the piece, or the way you're doing it, or feel that you're failing altogether, choose to behave celebratorily: clap your hands, cheer, laugh, hoot, whatever.

And if you become unsure of either yourself or your accomplishments, instead of letting it pass by, make up a gentle soft-shoe routine, or a little finger-tapping or head-rocking movement.

Remember, any of these choices of anti-behaviors must be based on you, your feelings—your own estimate of success or failure, as you act the material. If your feelings should change while you are acting out one of these opposites, you have to keep up with and admit the change.

As with all exercises, you shouldn't just behave momentarily. Sustain whatever movements you start, lengthen them, strengthen them, involve yourself in them, and if you get lost or too confused to know which of your feelings are the truest, simply let that old soft-shoe routine take over.

You'll find that many of your "opposite" choices of behavior become a better means of expressing what's been going on than your first impulses. This is another measure of how habitual your responses have become.

Even without the structure of the above exercise, it's never a bad idea to try out some opposites while rehearsing a piece. Where you presume the character would be inclined toward generosity, try some stinginess; when the script seems to call for a patriotic response, let yourself become cynical; in a love scene, consider leaving during it. All these experiments will either open you to fresher and more insightful possibilities, or they'll confirm your initial approach. That's what rehearsals are for: to explore, to find out. And since each of us is trying to enter the realms of beings and situations far from our own, our first, habitual responses can be very misleading.

I've asked actors: "Which would you rather be—an onrushing, ever-changing series of impulses, thoughts, and feelings that need to be channeled, or a cool, calm, and collected reservoir of comfortable sensations that keep you safely preserved at all times?" Every actor has chosen the onrushing stream. That seems to be the natural human response.

But if controlling these ongoing floods of sensations sounds complicated (controlling them, *not squelching them*), remember that people everywhere, in every culture, have learned that flooding can be harnessed. Huge bodies of water can be diverted and channeled into useful purposes such as electricity, irrigation, reservoirs. It's far better to conduct these waters than to stop them.

The same is true for impulses within us. It takes far too much effort to suppress what we feel and think when simply conducting these thoughts and feelings elsewhere can achieve so much.

If a car is impeding your progress going down a curving mountain road, going even slower than the posted minimum speed, you would tend to become really annoyed; you would feel you had every right to honk at the driver or even tailgate him to force him to go faster. But if that slow driver were to lose control and topple off the roadway, your angry feelings would immediately undergo a drastic change. Anger and frustration would become guilt, bewilderment, and compassion. Where did those angry feelings go? Did they evaporate? Were they suppressed? You can say they've been replaced. The point is, they've moved. Some process of conducting has taken place.

When you go to visit a loved one or a friend who is seriously ill in the hospital, your feelings of concern and worry may be predominant, but the moment you enter the sick room you can change those thoughts and feelings into a show of encouragement and happy support.

It is a very convenient human quality to be able to move our feelings elsewhere, not repress them or squash them, not even deny them, just move them.

If we could consider ourselves as instruments by which we conduct thoughts, feelings, and actions that are more valid for the roles we are playing than just for ourselves, we would find access to far more varied expression than we accept in our own everyday lives.

Even if we presume some of our own impulses are wrong for the character we're working on, we would have the means to conduct these impulses elsewhere for the time being. In life we are able, under changing circumstances, to easily and quickly alter a response. Why not as actors?

In chemistry, a catalyst is an ingredient that either speeds up or slows down a reaction, without undergoing any change itself. What a marvelous concept for actors. Whenever there is an obstacle or distance between you and the role, a search for the proper catalyst is all that's needed. You needn't berate yourself, think of yourself as inadequate, or think of the part as beyond you. It's simply that you haven't yet found the proper catalyst. And a catalyst for an actor can be anything: a person, a place, a color, an action, an attitude. Imagining one of these choices as a catalyst frees you from being right or wrong about your choice. You are free to try it out and see.

If you are having trouble behaving luxuriously, imagine yourself wearing nothing but cashmere (if you think, as most people do, that cashmere epitomizes luxuriousness). The imagined cashmere clothing becomes your catalyst. If your character needs to feel serene or safe, imagine a grandparent hugging and caressing you as a child. If you're supposed to be expansive with your voice and body, think of being on a beach talking to someone out in the surf.

In silent films (you know, in the real old days), the director, for love scenes, would often have a chamber group play appropriate music just out of camera range to inspire the actors. Not a bad idea nowadays, either. To put yourself in a romantic or seductive state, you don't need the musicians to actually be present; just imagine whatever music might inspire you.

If your love is of the sweet and innocent kind, you might picture your pet cat or dog. If you're required to be bereft and heartbroken, you can imagine that same pet having to be put to sleep. The audience will attach your emotional responses to those of the character's. They will never know what you were thinking of to achieve those results.

There is an enormous difference between our reactions to circumstances and the perceptions we are objectively capable of bringing to them. It takes almost nothing to get a person to react. If someone were to slap you in the face, you would most likely flush with anger and want to retaliate. If someone were to shut you up in a dark hot room for an hour or so, you would probably end up sweating and frightened. If a nice-looking stranger were to stop you on the street and ask for directions, you would probably give them.

But if that first someone had hit you because you were hysterical, you would have had to realize that the slap was not meant to hurt you but to bring you to your senses. When an attendant shut you up in a darkened steam room in a health club, you actually paid him money to make you sweat. If there'd been a series of muggings in your neighborhood, you would think twice about talking to the stranger.

Suppose while you were shopping you found yourself in a violent disagreement with a salesperson about your taste in clothes. You would feel perfectly justified in getting furious and leaving. But if on your way out of the store the manager apologized and then explained that the employee who argued with you had just been notified that he had incurable cancer, your reactions would change considerably.

Those initial feelings—our reactions—are a product of our habitual selves. We need to persuade ourselves that we have the choice to behave differently. It's like making yourself ask, "Now that I've been slapped, what could that have been about?" Or, "Now that I've been shut up in this hot, darkened room, what good use can I make of it?" Or, "Do I need to know any more about this stranger before talking to him?"

If, when you opened your mail in the morning, you found an unexpected refund check from the Internal Revenue Service for several thousand dollars, it's not enough just to say you'd be happy. What might the rest of your day then be like? What might you do differently? How might you greet and treat those around you? How might you view the world?

Suppose, on the other hand, when you opened your mail there was a bill from the I.R.S. demanding several thousand dollars in back taxes. Then what might the rest of your day—or week—or life—be like? You wouldn't begin to cover the territory just by reacting with bitterness or anger.

A habitual greeting by relatives at a family gathering may make us feel warm and secure; it doesn't enlarge our knowledge of one another. The same is true of acting a role. If we bring only our customary, habitual reactions to the part, we won't be any wiser about our characters; instead, we will have reduced that character to what our own habits and reactions dictate.

Every good actor wants to journey into new worlds when working on a part. Why bring along only old baggage on your trips?

Each of us has originalities within us. Each of us has the capacity to recognize originality in others. We need to learn to be both objective and empathic when relating to characters. We need to encourage ourselves to see life through their eyes with their attitudes—even those we dislike—and then we have to give ourselves permission to think and feel as they do.

When we're children, we want the loved ones around us to stay the same. But as we grow, we no longer want them to treat us as children. We want to be seen as individuals with our own desires and aptitudes, we want appreciation for our ideas, we want compliments for our accomplishments. None of us wants our epitaphs to be "She was always the same."

Why, then, bring that sameness to your acting? Get your habits out into the open where you can take a good look at them. You can always keep those you prefer. But the law of life is change. Either we become flexible and adaptable, or we atrophy. There isn't a great artist who ever lived who used the same techniques all his or her life; they all developed new attitudes and experimented with new forms. Should you do any less?

Situations

When actors read a script, the *first* ingredient they have to deal with is the words. But when authors write scripts, the *last* ingredient for them is the words. The ideas, thoughts, observations, experiences, and imaginings that are included in authors' characters and drive the plot have all occurred before and during the process of writing. Their very last act is committing to paper those words they have honed.

As actors, we have to work backward. We have to face those words on the pages as if they were merely the tips of acting icebergs. To plumb those icebergs' hidden parts, we need to separate them into areas of acting work: the text itself, the characters, and the situations.

Of the three, situation is the clearest to define and evaluate. And it's the most accessible to create. It doesn't even require words, only the use of our senses, our bodies, and our voices. Its results are quickly and objectively confirmable. And it is eminently gratifying because no one else but the actor is capable of creating it.

There are basically two kinds of situations: external, in which the physical circumstances are predominant, and internal, in which the event is determined by how an individual focuses thoughts and feelings related to the physical circumstances.

In the late 1950s, a theater company called the Berliner Ensemble became world famous for its dazzling productions and acting style. Their work was not dazzling in the glitzy Broadway-musical sense, but offered insightful and memorable vignettes of theatricalized human behavior. Theirs were epic productions, encompassing every human passion and conceit imaginable, combined with extraordinary physical production details. Actors, directors, critics, and audiences alike flocked to Berliner Ensemble productions to witness the marvels on stage.

A young director, dying to work with the Ensemble, wrote letter after letter asking to be considered. Finally, after months of frustration, he was invited to attend a rehearsal to be conducted by one of the Ensemble's younger directors, supervised by the master director-writer Bertolt Brecht. He was told to be on time, watch the rehearsal, then Brecht himself would talk to him.

The director arrived promptly on time. The entrance to the theater was unlocked. Inside, with only work lights on, a group of very young men were frolicking around the auditorium, telling jokes, chasing each other through the aisles, sometimes dashing on stage to take turns falling off a table, doing stunts with chairs, all in good humor, all in vigorous athletic competition.

In the semi-dark auditorium, the director perceived Brecht seated beside a younger man, chatting with him, occasionally observing the antics around them. At different times, a small group of the athletic men would swoop down upon Brecht and his companion and tweak them, sometimes verbally, sometimes physically, which Brecht and the other man seemed to accept graciously.

The invited director sat himself down at the rear of the auditorium, re-checked his watch for the time, then waited patiently for someone to acknowledge his presence or for the rehearsal to begin. Neither seemed to happen. More than an hour passed. The director's patience wore thin. Just as he was about to leave to look for someone on staff, the man beside Brecht stood up and called, "Enough. Take a break. Very good."

The young men scattered, most exiting offstage. Brecht looked about, spied the director, and called him forward. The director by now realized that all those running-around activities were the rehearsal itself. But of what? It didn't look to him like any play or any rehearsal he had ever seen.

In the course of a warm introductory conversation with Brecht, the director soon discovered that the young men he had seen, all actors in the company, were rehearsing a piece in which college students cavorted at a *rathskeller* by telling jokes, tweaking their teachers, and competing over who could fall off a table best. That's what they were assigned to explore in their rehearsals: not just once but many times. From the various improvisations the best choices would be selected and re-rehearsed to hone them to their optimum. The director had learned a very valuable lesson: *First the actor improvised the physical situation, then the characters and the scenes could take shape.*

Berliner Ensemble improvisation-rehearsals for a play could easily take six months or a year to explore. Stanislavski's Moscow Art Theater, Grotowski's Polish Lab Theater, the Group Theater in New York—indisputably among the great theatrical organizations of the twentieth century—all engaged in extensive improvisations for their productions.

Today, almost no one on Broadway, in regional theaters, in films, or certainly in television has the financial resources or time available for that kind of rehearsal. So it is more incumbent than ever for actors to learn how to explore through improvisation on their own.

I'm not talking about the kind of improvisations that are meant to demonstrate cleverness, to amuse, or to satirize. Those improvisations lead to glib solutions, not illuminations. I am talking about improvisations to explore the situations in the script (and, later on, the nature of the characters and their attitudes toward these events).

Long before I read of the Berliner Ensemble, one of the strangest, really silliest, experiences in my early training was in an improvisation class. The teacher was fond of group plots: We were all to imagine ourselves on a picnic in a park, and just as we were about to eat, a rainstorm wetted us out. Or we were at our first high school dance, and soon after finding a dancing partner we liked, we had allergic reactions.

This particular day, the suggested improvisation was that we were all bank tellers who had just finished a shift and were gathering for a coffee break when a fire broke out—and all the exits were blocked. When we reached this point in the improv, everyone began screaming, yelling, crying, and beating the walls. Except me—I fainted (not really, just acting).

The teacher stopped us. He pointed at me and said, "Why did you do that? Why didn't you try to get out?" My classmates stared. I hesitated, suddenly wary and confused. "Everyone else knew to call for help," the teacher continued, "why didn't you?"

"I guess my character was a coward," I replied.

The class laughed and so did my teacher. And I never chose to faint again. But of course, it bothered me. With that teacher, from then on, I did whatever I thought he wanted me to do when we improvised. After I left his class—very soon after the fainting incident—I reinvestigated the issue.

I began to realize that the teacher was trying to make us *react* to the situations, not explore them—and to react in only one way to each situation. He wanted us to dramatize the result of our reactions, not investigate the physical and emotional possibilities of the situation.

In the case of the fire in the bank, we first needed to assign ourselves various duties, then choose a time of day, so that we would know if we had just arrived or if it was close to quitting time. We would have had to know how we usually dressed, and what the climate conditions were inside the bank. We certainly would have to know the physical layout of the bank entrances, cubicles, stairwells, doors, exits, solid or glass partitions or walls, etc. And then we should have taken the time to improvise an ordinary day's activities before introducing the elements of the smell of smoke and the fire itself. All that would at least have given us a creative base from which to explore possible inner responses.

A few months after I left that improvisation class, I was cast in an Off-Broadway play, John Van Druten's *Young Woodley*. We had a spirited director, who excitedly told us that all our early rehearsals would be improvised—anything we thought of could be used. We were thrilled, and without further ado, he suggested we begin right away.

The play was set in a young man's boarding school in England. The director pointed to our acting area, and designated it as a kind of green room, a gathering place that the students used between classes. He told us to take whatever objects we wished with us—books, pencils, sticks to be used as canes, hats, cushions, whatever—and start improvising.

The other actors let out a sort of war-whoop and eagerly rushed to their "green room." I didn't. I watched for a few moments, trying to gather my thoughts and ideas, when I heard the director call, "Hold it, hold it everybody." They stopped to see what was wrong.

"Allan," the director asked, "what's the matter? Why didn't you join them?"

All eyes were on me. I thought back to that damn fire-in-the-bank improvisation, but this time I held my ground.

"Because I don't know yet if we're here before classes start—is it the beginning of a term or near the end, are we freshmen, do any of us know each other, are we all doing well in classes? How do we feel about our parents paying our tuition? Or are we on scholarship? Or are we orphans? If we don't set some of the things, I don't know what to improvise on except just generally flopping around trying to have a good time."

It was all said in a mouthful, almost in one breath, and I stopped, expecting to be fired (or at least reprimanded) on the spot. The director stared, looked toward the rest of the cast, smiled, shrugged, and said, "He's right. We've got to set some information here or what you come up with'll be pretty general. I promise you'll still have a good time, though," and he laughed. "C'mere, Allan, let's get together on this."

We all did. And our rehearsals were quite wonderful. We filled out a lot of those words in the script with behavior and attitudes and relationships we might never otherwise have found.

For every scene's situation, at least one *unwritten preceding* scene should first be explored by improvising.

Before the scene in which Lady Macbeth hears of her husband's encounter with witches, what has their life been like together? Have there been any other supernatural events? Does either of them ever use sorcery to help guide their activities? (Ronald Reagan heeded the advice of an astrologer, so God knows what the Macbeths may have used.) Were they a doting romantic couple, or were there already signs of a love-hate relationship before he went off to his latest wars?

How do you answer any of these questions? Try acting them out improvisationally.

That's what Geraldine Page did one day in a class. She improvised a scene in which Lady Macbeth was alone at night, reading a letter from her husband (which she had written herself). First she created the sense of night; she lit a candle and moved it around to help suggest the darkness just beyond its light. There were smells in the air that seemed to arouse her. She was dressed in a nightgown and robe, and as she responded to the scents in the air, her body began to move more sensuously. She took the already-opened letter from her robe's pocket and reread it. As she did, the sensuousness diminished, as if her husband's words were too serious, too constrained for her appetite.

In a while, as her restlessness increased, she began to walk about the room she had created, listening and looking, half-hiding as she established that no one was nearby. Then, with increasing furtiveness and excitement, she took a piece of chalk and drew a large circle on the floor. She gathered many candles, and placed them around the chalk circle as she began an incantation. As she lit the candles, her voice became more and more tense, her body swayed as if caught in some primitive tribal rite, and she began calling her husband's name—moaning it, wailing it, sending it out a long distance. Then she began to repeat "Hear me, want me, hear me, want me," her voice rising and falling, her body undulating and seeking, until in one final crescendo, she called out only the second phrase: "Want me, want me, want me!"

It was powerful, and clearly put into focus ideas Geraldine had been mulling over for the kind of life Lady and Lord Macbeth shared before the play actually began. We all wished it had become part of a production of the play. Instead, it remained an insightful sketch by a creative actress working on the role for her own artistic sake.

Understand, she didn't try to compete with Shakespeare's language in her improvisation, she chose only a few key words to speak, words that Lady Macbeth *might* have said.

If you want to improvise on any sequence of an author's, use as few words as possible. But if you really feel the absence of linguistic imagery, try speaking song titles, book titles, or even movie titles. They can be very expressive. And they will relieve you of the need to make up words of your own.

To improvise attitudes and responses of a character to a situation, some language is usually helpful. But to improvise and explore the physical details of a situation by itself, *no words* are necessary.

One of the ways for you to know how Willy Loman in *Death of a Salesman* carries his sample cases when he comes home late at night is to improvise carrying around suitcases of your own all day in the heat, or the rain, or the cold, up and down steps, into and out of your car, and so on.

When Anne Bancroft played Mother Courage on Broadway, it was long into rehearsals by the time the stage crew had a real loaded wagon for her to pull. And yet that's what the character was known for. So Anne came to rehearsals wearing extra tight suspenders to force her back and shoulders to feel the pressures she would when pulling a heavy wagon. She filled her shoes with very small pebbles to simulate the wear on Mother Courage's sometimes bare feet as she followed the army through every kind of terrain.

Even in more highly-stylized theaters in other countries, this kind of improvisation is used. Chinese classical acting students were required to walk barefoot in real snow to act the essence of cold on their feet in later productions.

It doesn't matter how lighthearted or complex a script is, it doesn't matter what the style is; your first explorations must include the details of the situations the characters find themselves in. Then *you* have to explore them. Only then are you free to choose the attitudes that your character will have toward a certain situation.

Say your character's situation is being on a boat that suddenly burst its hull in the middle of the night and begins to sink. You would first have to define the circumstances of this accident, and then try to create all the sensory elements that make up such an accident: the sound of the hull bursting, the voices raised because of it, the warning sirens, the lurches and listings of the boat, the smells of fire or smoke, the sight and sounds of passengers and crew scurrying about, the sudden taste of nausea or dryness in your mouth, the fluttering of your heart, the movement of your body as you try to find your way to a lifeboat—endless details without a word of dialogue.

Suppose the situation is a couple at the beach with their very young daughter—and the child is suddenly nowhere to be seen. There's no way in the world you would know how you might respond without first improvising what your life with that child had been like before the disappearance.

The physical circumstances of the beach can be, and should be, improvised separately: Where did you last see the child? Is she somewhere out in the water? Are there other children nearby that yours could be playing with? Should you call the child by name, and if you do, do you hear any reply?

There are so many ingredients in this situation that need your attention. As you follow them out in detail, your empathy will be aroused. Similar situations will flicker into your consciousness. Feelings will move through you. Then, and only then, will come the task of trying out different character responses. Will yours tend toward hysteria or suddenly become desperately logical?

There's a spare, sensorial short story by Ernest Hemingway titled "Hills Like White Elephants." In this story, a couple is waiting at a rail station in the Spanish countryside for the next scheduled train (to an unspecified city). They order drinks from the station restaurant; it is unusually hot, and their wait is long. At one point, their eyes are drawn to the hills nearby, which look to one of them like white elephants. We learn from the dialogue that the woman is pregnant and that the couple is on their way to her having an abortion. Hemingway never tells us explicitly how the two actually feel toward one another or the impending operation. It's an absorbing story nonetheless, and wonderfully open to interpretation of the characters' feelings and attitudes. It's also a perfect way to illustrate that until you can create the sense of a rural train station, the waiting for a train, the heat, the accumulation of drinks, and the weight of facing the coming abortion, you have no right to try being frivolous about the situation—or solemn, optimistic, or anything else as the character.

How do you create the reality of an imaginary boat crossing the horizon in front of your character's eyes—before you concern yourself with whether the character feels saddened, exhilarated, lost, or whatever? How do you create the flight of a bird around you, whether outdoors or in a room? There's a huge difference between a situation and a character's responses to such a situation.

In the case of the bird or the boat crossing in front of you, the methodology is the same. You just follow the flight path of a selected bird with your eyes and/or you mark out the movement of a boat across the horizon. Whether you actually see the bird or the boat is immaterial. You oblige yourself to follow the logic of the creature's or the object's movements, and thereby create for your audience—and yourself—a pattern of behavior or movement that is true to the creature or object chosen.

Using this same logic will create similar truths for any situation.

What we all need to learn and relearn is that actors at their best are capable of illuminating their roles more than the writer's words alone can. Volumes and volumes have been written over the centuries to try to analyze the character of Hamlet, yet one performance of that role by an Edmund Kean or a John Gielgud far surpasses any verbal description.

To become that incisive and illuminating, it's not necessary for an actor to be an intellectual pundit, a therapist, an analyst, or a critic. It is necessary, though, that the actor devote herself to scoring the role with finite details that lay out all the governing and appropriate physical and emotional circumstances of the situations and events which the character finds herself in.

If a director decides to set *A Midsummer's Night Dream* in a modern gymnasium, you should explore that environment before assuming what your character would or would not do in it. If the director wants *The Zoo Story* set in an army base in Louisiana, you need to spend time establishing that locale for your character, and the kind of life the character may have lived in it.

Whatever circumstances the script or the director may dictate, *we* must explore. We must allow our freshest, truest, most open selves to participate in these explorations. Then, and only then, do we have the artistic right to decide the attitudes for our characters to take.

Character

We all, actors and non-actors alike, learn by duplication. We learn the alphabet by duplication; the teacher draws a symbol on the blackboard, calls it "A," and makes us repeat it until we all sound the same. Buttoning a blouse, frying an egg—someone shows us the activity, we go over it until we know how. The greatest painters first study the techniques of prior masters, duplicate their techniques, then develop their own. Examples of inductive reasoning or deductive reasoning are given to us, examples are repeated until our minds absorb the patterns, and there we are, thinkers.

I'm talking about duplication, not imitation. For me, imitation is doing something the way *someone else* would do it. Duplication is you doing something that someone else does, but in your own way.

If you want a limp for your character (or if a limp is demanded by the script), *you* have to practice a limp until it becomes familiar enough for you to include it easily in your own activities.

If you want to sound like someone else—someone with a gravelly voice or a French accent—*you* have to speak with those vocal qualities.

If your character is generous and loving, *you* have to practice behaving generously and lovingly.

And you must do these things in public: at gatherings, the market, parties, on a date. Then you have to try out *attitudes toward life* caused by that limp, that change of voice, or that loving generosity. You have to determine the deprivations it might cause or the privileges it might gain you, how relationships might suffer or grow because of it, whether to act more the victim or the hero because of it.

Brick, a character in Tennessee Williams' *Cat on a Hot Tin Roof*, has broken his leg doing a drunken stunt. The fact that he can't walk well allows him to keep to himself, unquestioned and uninvolved.

The same is true for Laura, another Williams character, in *The Glass Menagerie*. Her braced leg and her sickliness help her avoid life's vicissitudes.

Now think of Richard III and his humped back, or Quasimodo in *The Hunchback of Notre Dame*. Richard tears into life and relationships using his deformity as a battering ram. He brings it up at every opportunity, at one time to excuse his excesses, at another as an invitation to lovemaking. Poor Quasimodo does just the opposite.

Love and generosity are much written and spoken of, but how many lovingly generous people do any of us know? Do these qualities become virtues or impediments as you practice them? Do they draw people to you, or alienate people because you've become too virtuous to be around?

Your character's physical traits and actions don't have to be extraordinary for you to find value in them. Captain Queeg's fondness for rolling steel balls in his hand in *The Caine Mutiny Court Martial* defines his character. When Marilyn Monroe, in the film *The Seven-Year Itch*, stands over an air vent to expose her legs, that action defines her character's pleasure. The clearer you make the physical evidence to define your character, the more fully you can rehearse your role.

And who is to judge you on these explorations? How will friends react seeing you with a sudden new limp? Or family? Or even strangers? (Actually, having a limp might be an interesting way to meet someone.)

The actor risks a great deal more than other artists in this arena. After all, how many writers would ever put anything down on paper if family, friends, or strangers were constantly looking over their shoulders as they wrote? Would painters risk a possible patron watching them progress through awkward sketches and the early stages of a painting to judge the finished work?

The actor must practice all ideas for his character, good or bad, in front of and on other non-actor human beings who, most of the time, no longer relish or even accept play-acting in their own immediate lives.

So most actors band together in classes, at one another's homes, or at actual rehearsals in order to test, shape, modify and search out their ideas. Gene Hackman, Dustin Hoffman, and Robert Duvall used to meet weekly at their shared apartment to demonstrate character walks, voices, and attitudes they had become interested in during the previous days. Robert De Niro still uses notebooks with jottings about his characters. He told *American Film*: "You see someone on the street and they have a certain walk, and you pick that up and say, 'Remember that walk,' and you'll just apply it automatically when you're doing a character."

It's an interesting thing: people usually want to know if actors are like the roles they play. Most actors (often the best) have always felt the need to be other than just themselves. As different as possible from their habitual selves. Give good actors a new nose out of putty, a stutter, a higher voice, a lower voice, an accent, a general's posture, a gangster's attitude, or the role of a princess/fisherman/prostitute, and they feel triumphant. Then no one will know who he or she is.

In life, these disguises are reserved for the realm of children (or adults at a costume party). A daughter wearing a mother's dress or shoes and playing at going shopping—or a son wearing his father's baseball cap, quoting his father, and playing at driving the car—is usually congratulated for play-acting, or at least smiled upon. No one suggests these children are being strange or irrational. Copying, mimicking, behaving like someone else, all are part of the growing process. Then one reaches a certain age, and acting like someone else becomes a sort of vice: something to be avoided, an unhealthy, almost abnormal undertaking.

Let's face it: the actor, a person who pretends to be someone else, is generally thought to be at least a little weird. Actors are often admired, often revered—and, yes, mimicked—but they're never really considered to be like the rest of mankind, like people who work for a living.

There is a continuing fascination with actors' behavior that seems to be bound in a mystery: how can grown-up human beings present themselves as all those other people? How do transformations that we all once played at as young children manifest themselves in these grown actors, while everyone else seems content to have only one persona for the rest of his or her life?

Whenever any of us, as adults in real life, behaves too far from our accepted norm, the usual response from family or friends is, "What's wrong with you?"

On a visit home for Mother's Day, if you turned your back on your mother when she opened her door, flung the flowers you brought her high into the air, and shouted "Hooray for Tinkerbell," your mother would have good cause to believe you were on drugs, mentally ill, or perpetrating a bad joke. But it certainly couldn't have been *you*.

Soon after that early Indian incident with my mother (see the "Inspiration" chapter), I won a role in a play at the Equity Library Theater in upper Manhattan, a wonderful theater run by Equity so its members could showcase themselves. It was a terrific part, but the character was practically a sadist. I was reluctant to invite my parents to the play, since they had never seen me behave anything like this character around the house. But of course, pride overcame anxiety: I was told by everyone connected with the production that I was exceptional in the role, and I believed them.

So one Sunday matinee, there my folks were, backstage after seeing the show. I introduced them to the company; they were very considerate and complimentary to everyone, including me. I volunteered to walk them to the subway entrance, since I had an evening show still to do.

Outside in the warm Sunday air, my Dad put his arm around me and said again how good he thought I was. My mother was silent, seemingly just enjoying my company. As we walked on, I mentioned that I had thought they might be upset seeing me play such a role. My father said, "No, no," immediately. My mother almost simultaneously asked, "Why would I think that?"

Chuckling a little, I said, "Well, you know, this character was pretty nasty. You've never seen me act anything like that before."

Mother replied, "You were very good, I mean it." My father quickly agreed.

I stopped them on the sidewalk and said, "Come on, Mom. This guy was really bad. Didn't you think I was pretty evil up there?"

"Well..."—a longish pause—"yes, sure you did some bad things, but underneath we could all see you had a good heart." Thank you, Mom.

How to be interesting and imaginative about choices for a character?

Start with simple, familiar activities. Like writing a letter. Gather two sets of writing materials at a table or desk. And two chairs, spaced apart. Separate the writing materials, one batch in front of each chair. Sit in one of the chairs. Pick someone you know to write a letter to. Try to surround yourself sensorily with the qualities of the place and time you've chosen: is it when you're left alone in your home, or when everyone else is asleep? Do you drink while you write? How are you usually dressed? If it's summer, do you write near an open window? Pick a time of day or night you would tend to write such a letter. Think over what you've been doing with your life since you were last in touch with this person you're writing to, and what this person means to you.

Then begin your letter. After a time, when you feel involved in the activity, leave off and move to the second chair. Use the separate piece of paper. Think about your character. Pick someone either written about in the script, or imagined, to whom the character might write. Pick a place and time of day or night in which the character might be writing. Try to surround yourself with the sensory qualities of the time and place you've chosen for the character, and begin the new letter.

After a time, when you feel involved in this activity, leave off, return to the first chair and your own letter. After another little while, change to the character's chair and the character's letter, only this time, while you are in the character's chair and circumstances, allow yourself to remember your own letter, and let some of your thoughts and feelings from that letter join with the character's.

Again, after a few minutes, switch back to your own chair and while you continue your own letter, allow some of the character's thoughts and circumstances to mix with your own.

After three or four of these changeovers, you'll find that you and the character are mutually writing both letters, and you will have crossed a threshold that has kept you and the character separate.

It's like shaping a figure eight out of two adjoining circles.

The same process and principle can be applied to endless activities of the character's: telephone calls, writing a will, preparing a meal, singing a song, doing a monologue, and so on.

Always begin with your own circumstances, then shift to the character's, then back again, and only then do the mixing.

To alert yourself to additional, unexpected ideas for your part, I have another exercise to suggest. Before I describe it, I want to assure you that although it sounds complicated and unwieldy, it works unbelievably simply.

Pick one true physical fact about yourself, e.g., you're wearing new shoes, your hair needs washing, you're still living with your parents. Next, choose one physically untrue thing about yourself (the wilder the better), but make sure it doesn't relate to the true thing you already picked. For instance, if your choice of the true thing was your hair needs washing, don't pick having two heads for the untrue thing (save the two heads for another time; it's a good one).

The two choices should be nowhere near each other in physical proximity. And avoid using a subjective evaluation such as you're too thin. (I'd have to ask, too thin for whom? On the Richter scale of thinness, are you a nine or only a six compared to someone starving in Ethiopia? Stick to physical facts.*)*

Okay. After the physically true and untrue choices, ask yourself to pick something you wish were physically true, or truer, about you. Like you wish you were three inches taller. Or you wish you had a size 36C bust. Or you wish you had enough money to feed all the homeless. Or you wish you were a terrific basketball player.

Repeat your three choices to yourself to make sure you remember them clearly.

Now start singing a song, any old song. Or an old monologue you know well without struggling for the words. Don't fuss over the song or the speech, they're merely there for you to play with. As you go through the piece—without planning anything ahead—leave yourself open to any physical impulse or idea that's based on any of your three choices, and carry it out as you continue the song or speech. Don't jump from one to another of your choices, and don't force yourself into having impulses. You can repeat the song or speech several times if necessary, and just carry out any behavioral impulse that springs up in you from any of those three physical choices. Sometimes do them in slow motion. Let these new impulses mix in with whatever you're saying or singing, and make your speaking or singing resonate with the energies in these new actions; if you find yourself jumping up and down, let your voice go with the movements. If the impulse is to behave threateningly—or lovingly—put these qualities into your voice.

And if you really enjoy any of these new impulsive behaviors, let yourself repeat them, but always remain open to newer ones.

When you have done this part of the exercise for a little while, take a breather. But don't puff anything away. Don't sigh to relieve yourself; don't settle yourself or get comfortable. Stay poised and ready to reinvolve yourself. Sift over the sensations that have been stirred up inside you. Gather them. Think over some of the things you did as you followed out those three choices.

Now consider the character you're working on. Pick something physically true about him. Make sure it's factual; make sure this physical characteristic is mentioned in the script. Then pick a physically untrue choice for the character. This one you'll have to make up from whatever you know about the character. And after that choice, use your imagination to pick something you believe the character would wish were physically true, or truer, about himself. Again, all three choices should have no physical proximity to one another.

And now go through your same song or speech from earlier, only this time let the three choices you just made for the character influence what you do. Without any planning. Just let the three images play in your mind as you speak or sing, and act upon whatever impulses pop up inside you even if they overlap or mix.

By the way, an important stipulation: if any impulse of violence of any kind arises from this or any other exercise, don't literally carry it out, act it out. If you feel the urge to break a piece of furniture or hit someone, pantomime it with full force and sound in the direction of the furniture or your fellow performer. There's no need to actually strike. Save that for when a director is present and encourages it—or when they hire a stuntperson.

When you've gone through the song or monologue using the character choices, take another short breather. Again, don't puff any of your feelings away. Sift over your new sensations and behaviors.

*Accumulate them. Compare them to those you gained when using
only yourself.*

*And now, with all six choices in mind (that's right, keep six in the
air, like a good juggler), pick a song the character might sing. Think it
over, you'll find a song that fits. Or use a speech of the character's. Or
a hunk of dialogue you've already memorized. Go through that piece,
only this time, leave yourself open to impulses based on any of the
physical choices, yours or the character's. Mix 'em and match 'em.
Don't order them around to fit anything in the words, let them find
you while you're talking or singing, and let them operate on you. Do
this for a while, sometimes changing your choices, sometimes keeping
them, and you'll soon find yourself coming up with a great new batch
of surprises to use for the role you're working on. And I mean this for
any role: Elizabethan, Chekhovian, modern, avant-garde, or comedy-
improvisational.*

You can only find true empathy with another person if you
include yourself. You mustn't disappear, you must be a part of the
proceedings. After all, when an adjustment has to be made during
rehearsal or performance, who does it, you or the character?
When the director takes you aside, whom is he or she talking to?
Who gets the credit—or the blame—for your performance on
stage or on screen? Not the character.

Do you ever read epitaphs or obituaries? They can be remarkable. In a few succinct images or descriptions, a whole life can be
summarized. Try this for a part: Write out an epitaph for the character you are working on, e.g., "Penny-pinching, obstinate, but
likes dogs." Then act out those things. Take those qualities and
attitudes with you to the supermarket, or the bank, or on a family
visit, and live up to what you've written for the character. (By the
way, I've often found that when I tell friends or family in advance
that I'm working on a role, I can get away with almost any kind
of behavior without scaring them away.).

Practice those qualities and *you are living the life of the
character.*

When you're stuck even for basic qualities about the part,
choose three or four other characters who are nothing like yours.
If you're working on Lady Macbeth, pick Juliet, Scarlett O'Hara,

Snow White, Zsa Zsa Gabor. Write out qualities, characteristics, and attitudes of each of these four women, and in no time, by comparing their descriptions to each other, you will be able to define things to work on for your part..

Even when you have good ideas for a character, something may be hindering you. Some years ago, I was called to read for a role in Clifford Odets' *The Country Girl*, which was already weeks into rehearsal. The actor playing the part of the director, Bernie Dodd, was not doing well. I came in excited because I was dying to do the role. I got it, and was immediately thrust into long rehearsals with the other actors who treated me kindly, but somewhat like a bump on their log. I had put all my energies into getting the part. Now, having won it, my lack of preparation showed. I began to flounder, trying to prove myself quickly but lacking details to work on. The director was not much help.

As we approached the first performance, I panicked, realizing I was unready. I knew I was equipped to do the part, I just didn't seem to know how. I sat in the back of the theater trying to puzzle things out when I suddenly realized everything that was happening to *me* was central to Bernie's dilemma in the play. He was ambitious. He had the capacity to be a terrific director, but something was holding him back. He had chosen his situation and was now desperately trying to live up to his role as director. He was in turmoil over his expectations, just as I was over mine.

So he and I were actually now equals, brothers in misery. Wonderful. But what do I act? Another thought (just like the one during the private dancing moment I had done years earlier at the Actors Studio) struck me: Act what I *wished* I could do in the role, just as Bernie wished he could fulfill himself. I stormed out on stage and acted everything that had built up inside me during rehearsals—the frustrated desires, the hopes and dreams I had for my performance, anything and everything I wanted to create for Bernie. And I took off like a rocket. Every performance.

Here's another variation on this idea. I was directing an actress in a play set in a small town in rural Oregon, where her character was someone always hired to sing at funerals, because she sang so well. There were other more important facets to this character, but unfortunately the actress thought of herself as a terrible singer, so all other considerations were put on hold until we solved the singing dilemma.

I said "Okay. *You're* a terrible singer; *she's* a wonderful singer, and there's no way in the world we're going to be able to turn you into a marvelous singer in our short rehearsal period. But what kind of singer do you think she is? Dramatic? Wailing? A blues singer? Now why don't you instruct the rest of the cast in her kind of singing? You conduct them."

That, the actress believed she could do. In a few minutes, she had roused the rest of the company to heights of dramatic singing, and in the process of guiding them, she became totally involved. Then I said, "Now you just sing like that." She did. And she became quite radiant in the role.

Laurence Olivier did a remarkable thing on Broadway in the play *Becket*. He had been acting the role of Becket while Anthony Quinn was doing the king. Quinn was very well-cast—he was crude and rough, and he was good. Olivier was very effective in his role, too. Then Quinn had to leave the cast, Arthur Kennedy was brought in to play Becket, and Olivier switched to the role of the king, a part almost everyone thought he was wrong for.

I had to return (along with hundreds of actors and audience members) to see what he did. Oh, was he brilliant! Olivier epitomized in his performance what people mean when they talk about the differences between English and American actors. He made choices that illuminated the mind and soul of the king—and he executed them terrifically—but he never needed to convince us that he *felt* what he did.

The king was an extravagant and outrageous character, motivated by ego and machismo. In a very early scene, when he comes to test his friend Becket's loyalty, he seizes upon the presence of Becket's mistress, a lovely young woman sitting silently playing the lute, and demands *her* as a sign of this loyalty. That's what the scene called for.

When Quinn played the King and did the scene he was loud and demanding, and the request for the woman came as an afterthought, a smart-alecky test of Becket's fealty.

By comparison, from the moment Olivier's king entered Becket's chamber, he couldn't take his eyes off the beautiful

woman, who never deigned to notice him. While he was addressing Becket (Kennedy), Olivier pressed his attentions on the
woman. In between the lines of the script he cooed and coaxed
the damsel, mouthing what must have been vividly obscene
words in the ears of the lady, for she turned beet-red on stage the
night I saw them. When she still refused to acknowledge his presence, in a fit of rage he pointed witheringly at the woman and
growled "I want her!"

What a great choice to demonstrate the king's ruthlessness and
need for power over everyone. It would have been easy to play
the scene only the way the lines seemed to suggest. Olivier
turned the sequence into a revelation about the character.

Here's another instance of the difference between the two
actors. At the end of the first act, during a drinking scene with his
generals and hangers-on, Quinn, as the king, became drunker and
drunker, angrier and angrier, until he called out the final words of
the act—"Becket! Becket!"—like a frustrated bear of a man
demanding loyalty.

When Olivier played the king, by the time he reached this
scene he was a man who knew he was losing an empire. He
drank to drown his sense of failure. He railed at his generals,
insulted them for their ineptitudes and disloyalties by spilling
liquor on them, spat at them, and beat them away from the table,
a crude and ruthless tyrant exerting power in the only ways he
understood.

Finally, having punched, spat, and doused his men with physical and verbal onslaughts, he dismissed them, not in anger but
sadly, acknowledging their limitations as they left. Then he lay
down at the edge of the stage's apron, upside down, and cried
out "Becket! Becket!," screaming the name of his one true friend,
like a child bereft of all his senses, terrified of his future. And as
the curtain fell, Olivier, still crying out, was dragged away by his
feet, just before the curtain hit the stage.

The mixture of exquisite vulnerability and crudeness created by
Olivier for the king throughout the play was indelible. There was
no question that Quinn looked more fitting for the role, but
Olivier's choices of behavior illuminated the part. He made his
choices and lived up to them courageously. Whether I believed

his performance was organic that night or not was immaterial; he inspired me to feel and think about his character, and thereby to understand him. Truly remarkable acting.

(To give Quinn his due, I don't believe even Olivier could have given as grand or true a performance as Quinn did in *Zorba the Greek*. That was a great film performance.)

With all that having been said, I would like to raise another issue about acting—and truth. When you take an oath as a witness in a courtroom you have to swear "to tell the truth, the whole truth, and nothing but the truth." But that truth invariably turns out to be factual truth: "Where were you standing when the car hit the woman? What happened next?"

When you gaze into the worried eyes of your doctor and say "Tell me the truth," does the physician tell you what's really in store for you, or only that portion of her diagnosis that she feels relatively sure of?

When you're leaving a party that's been a failure, do you tell your host your true feelings, or lie and say what a good time you had?

We always tell selective truths to people around us. Sometimes it's because it serves as protection for ourselves, sometimes it seems to help others. In other words, we lie in a good cause. We lie because it's *for* a good cause.

In an accident, if a child were to be hurt beside us, no matter how terrible our own pain, most of us would be capable of denying our own difficulties in order to assure the child that everything was going to be all right.

We have the will, and we have the power, to choose to lie about ourselves in order to do someone else good. Why shouldn't the same principle apply to acting? If the cause is good, and you behave other than, even opposite to, the way you actually feel, who would call you to account?

Some actors and acting teachers refer to this sort of adjustment with the phrase "as if." You behave toward your host at the party as if everything is fine. To reassure the child in the automobile accident, you would behave as if you were not hurt. I have no quarrel with this approach; I've used it beneficially from time to time in the past. However, more often, it has not engaged my faculties and feelings as creatively or as deeply as I would have wished.

At the end of four years playing a well-loved character on a soap opera, I was going to be "killed off." (I was leaving to teach at Yale University and act at the Repertory.) The writers chose a heart attack as the cause of my demise. My dying scenes (which went on for weeks) were well-written, and I wanted to give them my all. I began by using the magic "as if." Helped by a doctor friend, I went over all the physical details that a specific kind of heart attack would generate, and practiced as if those things were happening to me.

When I then tried to apply the as-if idea to the sequences of dying that followed the heart attack, I found myself sort of making believe I was dying—like I used to do in my childhood made-up gunfights. I felt too much like a pretender. Too much on the surface.

So I turned it around. I said to myself, "You lucky son of a bitch, look how healthy you are. You can play two whole games of softball in 93-degree heat and still feel ready to go on. You've got two great young sons who love you. You're earning a really good living. Your mother's finally proud of you..." I went on and on in my mind about all the wonderful things around me at that time in my life until I felt overflowing with the rich, warm sensations of being alive. I then asked myself what my life would be like without any of those things—no children, no softball games, no job, no parental approval.

The responses that came up in me because of these questions gave me dimensions and textures of thought and emotion that I was able to bring to the role, and created far more for me than merely behaving "as if" my life were coming to an end.

As a matter of fact, once you know how you feel and choose to behave in an opposite way, couldn't that be construed as another form of truth? In order to lie you, must be in touch with the truth—or you wouldn't know what to lie about.

It's like someone saying to you (for whatever reasons), "From now on you mustn't think about any rhinoceros." How can you then not think of rhinoceros? You have to make sure you're not thinking of the creature, and the only way to make sure is to refer to one—and then move your thoughts away. As a child, every time my parents or a teacher admonished me not to do or think something, I'd think about it even more. So did all my friends. That seems to be a principle of human nature. Why not take advantage of it, and actively accept this form of lying?

An actor must know in advance (and I hope, will check to be sure) that the knife that stabs him on stage or in film is a false one, a prop. Does he then not lie in a good cause to act the character's death? And is he not freer then to "die" on stage? When a couple is married on stage (or in film) and they promise to love one another forever, do they go home together after the show? Are the actors not freer to commit themselves to each other because these truths are lies? Why try to *be* a madman when you're acting? Far easier and more adventurous to acknowledge that you're not mad—list and practice all the attitudes and actions that prove you're not mad, then choose to behave the opposite. You'll then be freer to try anything that you can think of for the role.

I created the part of a rich, complex character in a play called *Are You Now or Have You Ever Been...* by Eric Bentley at the Yale Repertory Theater. I worked very hard on the part because physically the character seemed so unlike me; yet I believed I knew his interior being well. The man was pudgy, had difficulty fitting into his collar, wore thick eyeglasses, spoke in a husky New Yorkese voice, and was afflicted with facial tics. He was also very witty.

I was slender, had 20/20 vision, spoke in a well-modulated voice with only a slight New York accent, and had no perceivable tics anywhere. I was also witty, so the wittiness I didn't worry about.

It was obvious that I couldn't quickly transform my thin frame into a heavy one (nor did I want to). And I knew I'd look silly trying to pretend I was fat. The essence of the character's fatness was that he was uncomfortable in clothes. So I bought a shirt to wear that was two sizes larger than my neck, I had a jacket tailored so that one sleeve was longer than the other, and I wore jockey underwear a size too small. If he was uncomfortable being too fat in clothes, I was going to be uncomfortably too thin.

Then instead of blinding myself with an actual pair of thick-lensed glasses, or trying to find a prop pair of clear glass just to have them on, I decided to go without any glasses at all, and tried to behave the way someone who relied on glasses would behave if he'd lost the glasses or had inadvertently left them behind. I began to alternately squint and widen my eyes fairly regularly.

I then added a few assorted facial tics. But what was to be the basis of this "tic-ing" behavior? It seemed to me that tics—anyone's tics—are like short-circuits in the nervous system: muscles jump involuntarily. As I observed my own physical structure, I was aware that I, like every other human being, was a mass of nerve impulses going on not all at once, but often: itches, dry-nesses, sniffles, coughs, toe wiggles, finger waggles and scratchings, leg shifts, arm shifts, neck shifts—you name it, my body was doing it, though it never took the form of tics. Energy is energy, so I decided that whenever I became aware of wiggles, or nerve impulses, or anything of the kind anywhere in my body, I would substitute a tic somewhere on my face. They became "real" tics because they were based on physical responses happening to me. I simply chose to "lie" about their placements.

This is one of the central ideas behind all great acting: actors, through force of will, discernment, and imagination, are able to transform their own beings into a body of movements, sounds, and feelings that convince an audience that they are other people. To accomplish this, actors always search for what is truest to their characters. That has never meant that the actor has to literally experience what the character goes through.

A young actor in a class did a love scene. He was in anguish most of the time. When the scene finished, the teacher asked the actor what he was working on.

"Love. This guy is crazy about this woman."

The teacher said, "But you were in pain all the way through."

The actor practically yelled his reply. "That's love, man. That's the way I always love. I gotta suffer or I know I don't mean it."

The teacher pondered a moment. "In this scene, the character is exhilarated about being in love. Your partner even has a line where she asks you why you are laughing. You never even smiled."

"How could I?" the actor countered. "It hurt too much."

"Then forget about love and find something else that makes you feel happy."

The teacher made no bones about where she stood on the matter—and neither do I. There is no contest between which comes first artistically, the actor's reality or the character's. But that doesn't mean the actor's truth should be denied or suppressed; it simply may have to be channeled, or parked. And if shifting your actual feelings and impulses in order to give life and truth to those of your character goes too much against your grain, just remember the words of Michael Gambon. This protean British actor told *The New Yorker* that the key to all character work is "finding the way the person is."

After a few years of recording renown, and a couple of outstanding acting performances, Barbra Streisand—at the time, still a young actress-singer—was in the running for the starring role of Fanny Brice in the Broadway production of *Funny Girl*. Her chief competitors at that time were Anne Bancroft and Carol Burnett, two older and much more experienced actresses, each of whom could command a far greater advance ticket sale than the relatively unknown Barbra.

She had already auditioned three times for Jerome Robbins, the director at that time, and Ray Stark, the producer. Robbins remained dubious of her capabilities for the role, and asked for a fourth audition. This time he made a specific demand: Barbra had to demonstrate that she had the maturity necessary to fulfill this very wide-ranging role (Fanny Brice ages from seventeen to almost forty in the show).

Though Barbra had studied with me for two years, and had been coached by me for an earlier Broadway musical, we had been out of touch for a while. Robbins' demand made her call.

She told me that she really hadn't felt the need for help during the first three auditions, but now she was stuck. She was to return the next day for her crucial and (hopefully) final audition. Was I available that evening to work with her? I said yes, and then she told me what she was supposed to bring in.

I couldn't believe it. "You want me to help you become more mature overnight?"

"Yup," she said. (We often communicated in short sentences.) Pause. Pause. "Well?" she asked.

I sighed deeply. "All we can do is try," I replied. "What time?"

It was already late afternoon. By early evening, after a light dinner, I was still puzzling over the task I'd accepted. I thought of people I'd known or seen or read about who embodied that curious characteristic, maturity, then I made myself remember characters in life and books and films who were clearly immature. And then I tried to match them up against each other, trying to perceive the essential attitudes and behaviors that seemed to separate them.

I made a list, and thought about ways of conveying those capacities and qualities to Barbra so that she could act them. I was also prepared to ask her which people she considered mature, and suggest she act like one of them.

By the time I arrived at her apartment, I felt somewhat armed with possibilities, but I was still trepidatious about her executing any of my choices. She was, after all, only nineteen.

Barbra greeted me at the door, and I could tell immediately from the mixed look of consternation and relief on her face that she'd already exhausted her own acting possibilities for the next day's audition. But we went over some of them anyway. She had tried very hard to tangle with the role, yet this need to be more mature had defeated her. She was pliant and vulnerable with me—but she'd run out of steam.

We talked over a number of possible people for her to try to be more like, but I could tell this approach was not going to be fruitful. Barbra had already half-convinced herself she might indeed be too young to achieve sudden and real maturity.

As we muddled everything over, I was looking around the room. My eye caught a picture she had on the wall. It was a print of a painting by Rembrandt in which a young peasant girl is hoisting her skirt just above water level as she dips her feet in a stream. In the background on one side of her was a small village; on the other side was a landscape. The girl's eyes were focused on her hemline and the water.

I turned to Barbra and said, "Look at her. Is she mature? She's very young, but does she seem mature in the picture?"

Barbra gazed at the girl. "Yeah."

"How come?" I asked.

She looked some more, but her head began to shake with the answer "I don't know."

"Sure you do," I said. "Don't try to *react* to her. Just say what she's doing."

"She's dipping her feet in the stream. She's hiking her skirt so it doesn't get wet. I mean, that's all she's doing."

"That's right." I was excited for both of us. "That's *all* she's doing. She's not trying to tell us, 'Oh, what a relief that I can cool my feet.' She's not looking around to see if anyone's watching. She's doing only what's necessary to get her feet cooled."

"Right," Barbra exclaimed. Now she was jubilant. She repeated my thought to get it really firm. "*She's only doing what's necessary for that task.*"

"That's it," I said.

"Wow," she said, all lit up, gesticulating with her hands. I stopped her immediately.

"Was all your hands-jumping-around necessary for that realization?"

She quickly thought, shook her head, and said firmly, "No."

"Did you have to shake your head no, as well as tell me?"

She thought that one over, then without any accompanying physical gesture, she quietly answered, "No."

"That was lovely," I said.

She beamed and her head and shoulders started to roll with expression. I pointed to the movements as she began them, and she quickly relaxed out of them, still smiling.

"Are you still happy about your new revelation?" I asked.

She beamed more fully, and with the very slightest head movement, she said, "I sure am."

The rest of the evening, I followed Barbra about the apartment as she answered the phone, greeted her husband Elliott Gould, prepared a snack, and chatted with Elliott and me, and I continued to silently point out any unnecessary reactive behavior from her. She was terrific at catching most of it herself.

At one point, while she was busy in another room, Elliott (who knew I was Barbra's coach) half-whispered to me, "Allan, what's she doing? What'd you give her to work on?" He was enjoying himself when he asked.

"Why, how does she seem to be?" I answered. Clearly, as a fellow actor, he'd been trying to figure it out for himself.

"I don't know. Different—older."

"You've got it. That's what she's working on."

The idea intrigued him. "It's her," he said, "no mistake about that. But she's a more mature woman."

They all thought so, too, the next day at her audition. Robbins was flabbergasted at the change in her, and she passed that audition. (Just for the record, she endured three more before she actually won the role.)

Do you enjoy looking at paintings or photographs? Have you ever considered using any as an entree into the building of a character? I don't mean only in the way I just defined for Barbra and I don't mean by trying to imitate someone in the picture. And I also don't mean to base your use of a painting on whether or not you like it. To use a painting or a photograph creatively, your first task has to be to try to determine the attitudes toward life inherent *in the piece, regardless of your personal response to it.*

If you were to look at a child-like drawing of a purple pelican, outlined in red and orange, mouth agape, face determined, eye bright and unflinching, set against a dreamlike palm and sky, what might you think the artist has drawn this creature to express? "Never mind what's around you, use yourself boldly. Demand what you want, and don't take no for an answer." Those could be very provocative characteristics to use for a role—Maggie in Cat on a Hot Tin Roof, *Henry Higgins in* Pygmalion—*or*

for anyone trying to behave like Madonna. Take a good look at the picture: don't try be the pelican, just try to live up to what you perceive its attitudes are.

Look at this photograph. Two very young schoolgirls—uniformed, with a school logo on their hats, blue plaid dresses, jackets trimmed with blue and white—in the foreground. Three older, differently-uniformed girls are fuzzy in the background. Two of them are focused on the girls at the curb, the other is turned away, busy with something. The two younger girls are the major force in the photo. They are waiting at a curbside. One of them is crouching, calmly fondling a collared dog. The younger-looking girl stands prominently in the foreground, one hand clasped upon a very large shoulder bag, her wide eyes staring off in the distance, perhaps watching for a vehicle to pick them up. The overall color in the picture is blue; not only the girls' clothes, but even the sidewalk has a cool, grayish-blue tone. The girls' peach-pink complexions, and the dog's soft orange-pink and off-white coat, are a vivid contrast to the dingy details around them.

What does this picture say about life for these girls? The one girl cuddling the dog seems to be at peace with her wait. The standing girl is tense and unsure. She seems isolated, at one only with her own concerns. I could easily identify with her situation, sympathize and wish her well. I could definitely feel sorry for her, and could want one of those older girls in the background to come forward and cuddle her, as her curbside companion is cuddling the dog. But that's not what the photo says. *It's only what my subjective reactions to the girl bring up in me. I have to separate myself from these reactions and try to perceive ideas about how to live life.*

The girl clutching her bag may be insecure, but she's sure holding her ground. She's not crying. She's not feeling sorry for herself, why should I? She's stronger than my reactions would have made her. I might have turned her into a victim, which is exactly the opposite of what the photo shows. This kid's going to tough life out, hanging on with her fingernails if necessary, but she doesn't need or want soothing in this situation, she just wants her transportation. And she's going to stand right up there till it comes. Kind of indomitable. A lot of vulnerability in her, but not bent by it. She's alert, very hot-blooded— her face looks almost flushed—and see how her eyes have eyeliner around them. This girl wants to be noticed. She'll probably demand to be noticed.

Not a bad bunch of characteristics to pull from a single photo. You could use those qualities and attitudes for any number of roles, from Shakespeare's Desdemona to George Bernard Shaw's Cleopatra to Robert De Niro's Travis Bickle in Taxi Driver.

Here's another painting. I've had it a long time and have used it often: a lavender, pink-toned teenager, fist on hips, a swatch of hair damp and slightly wind-blown, a doll flopped over her arm, smiling face forward, wearing over-large reflective sunglasses, set against a garish sky and beach. Her body is forthright, her bikini top low-slung, her young nipple-protruding breasts almost unhidden, her slender hips and thighs barely contained by a sliver of a bikini bottom. She seems entirely available, except for the doll and her totally hidden eyes—Lolita incarnate.

But what's the idea? To lure young Playboy *readers-to-be? To rattle and shake up the settled lusts of older more established men? To make less well-endowed women feel jealous or threatened? Or is the theme of the painting closer to, "You can't always judge a book by its cover"? The young lady is quite pleased with herself. She can see us but we can only see her body. She has the power; we, her viewers, don't. Along with the doll, we have become her toys. "Think what you will, even do what you will," she seems to be saying, "My thoughts and feelings are mine alone. Enjoy yourself, buster; you're mine, too." Great attitudes and qualities to use for characters whose real lives stay hidden, like Orson Welles' Charles Foster Kane or Henrik Ibsen's Hedda Gabler.*

I've been giving you my own interpretation of these pictures. There are certainly others. All that's important is that you be able to back up your own definition of attitudes in any picture by the factual details that are in that picture. There is no right or wrong interpretation of these details. The attitudes toward life that you choose are to help you define your character and his or her way of life.

Let me throw in one more photo, a personal favorite of mine. It's a photo of a Barcelona rooftop —actually, only a detail of the rooftop, one small section of tiles and bracework almost devouring a round tower with a crazily cartoonlike minaret on top of it. Even the tile roof is strangely wavy, with an awkward knob-like binding. Far off in the background, just a piece of a standard twentieth-century apartment building is in view. The main colors in the photograph are the burnished golden copper tones of the tiled roof and tower, against a violet blue sky. Signs of ancient wear on the roof and tower are also prominent.

Why is it a favorite of mine? First, because this design is so unexpected (and I've learned to enjoy the unexpected in my acting work). Second, because it's unconditionally individual. There can't be another roof exactly like this one anywhere. It came roaring out of someone's imagination. It reminds me of a tale told of Leonardo da Vinci. In his day, there were many stories of prehistoric creatures, but not yet any substantial geological evidence. He was determined to make up his own creature, so he had the carcasses of every kind of dead animal avilable brought to him. He dissected and rearranged different parts of each until they formed an animal that lived up to the one he had imagined.

The rooftop design in this photo is like that creature to me. Each element of the structure seems representative of other building-works from centuries ago, but put together, they are unlike any architecture I've ever seen.

Then what about an attitude toward life based on the picture? To me, this picture says, "Dare to be different. Be true to any of your feelings. They all count. Do what you do vividly out in the open. Celebrate your life, don't try to mix in comfortably. Try things newly."

A pretty good recipe for characters from Mercutio to James Bond. And I mention these characters because they're very difficult to fulfill. Maybe a rooftop in Barcelona can be your inspiration when you find such a role.

For this book, I've deliberately chosen pictures that are, in themselves, undramatic. My point is that any visual image—a photo, a painting, a child's drawing, even a commercial illustration for a product—can be thematically exciting. You don't have to be in the presence of a master to kindle your own imagination.

Here's another idea for creating a character.

Sid Caesar, on his wonderful old TV series "Your Show of Shows," often acted out the life of an inanimate object. He would take a gum machine and act it being installed on a subway platform: a new, young, inexperienced, eager machine. He carried his body very rigidly but with his eyes and face always alive and human. You understood he was not a person, but an object with thoughts and feelings. He entered with his body at a slight angle to suggest he was being carried.

His eyes took in everything they could from that angle, and he made sounds and faces to express his delight and his anticipation at being of service. He suddenly stopped walking and up-righted himself. He made drilling noises, looked down at his feet, and moved them slightly up and down in conjunction with the vocal sounds, to suggest he was being bolted to a platform. He acted out a series of encounters: a pretty young woman passing by, the arrival and departure of a train, an older lady checking herself in his mirror. A man inserted a coin, Caesar made a gulping sound, took in the coin, lowered his outstretched hand to suggest the choice of a gum flavor, then vertically coiled and rolled his body, and triumphantly stuck out his tongue, which clearly became the gum itself. All this while his torso was rigid. He acted out the feelings he thought appropriate to the young machine, as well as whatever physical noises and head movements were necessary to clarify the outer actions. The climax of the story was the arrival of a young tough who, against Sid's best, frantic efforts, inserted a slug instead of a coin and jammed the poor machine. Jammed it so badly that a workman came, unbolted him, and took him away. It was very sad. And totally compelling.

Any of your imaginations can be sparked by investing a little time in such object improvisations: an old washing machine in a very kind household falling in love with a new, younger dryer; a leaf in a large family of leaves blown loose by a high wind—on the ground, alone and cut off from nutrients, the leaf slowly turning color and dying, only to be plucked up by a young girl out on a walk, who takes the leaf home to press it into a permanent place in one of her favorite books.

I was given a featured role in a very difficult play, *The Courageous One*, Off-Broadway in New York in the late 1950s. Many of the characters, including mine, were suffering emotionally. The director, a colorful and persuasive Russian woman, wanted a sense of exhausted physical deprivation as well. She said she wanted us to act as if we were among the last survivors of a Nazi concentration camp. My fellow actors took her suggestion enthusiastically, and in no time were busily improvising their characters on that basis. I felt stuck. The director quickly noticed my reluctance and came over for a quick conference. I told her that the concentration camp idea was too horrible for me to work on, too frightening. She tried to assure me, to ease my apprehensions, to convince me to "just give it a try."

I did try. Hard. But no matter how I presented it to myself, at that time in my life the last thing in the world I could get myself to empathize with was being in a concentration camp. I felt terrible. I had a rich part and I was unable to bring it to life. I couldn't even focus on it creatively.

One evening, after another frustrating day's rehearsal, I was walking along Columbus Avenue. I'd taken the night off to see a movie, and I was window shopping. I suddenly stopped in front of a lamp repair store. A dark, seedy one. I saw all those lamps full of dust, some with their wiring pulled out, some with no bulbs or shades. I just stood there staring. Published photos of concentration camp survivors began mixing in my mind with the look of the neglected and misused lamps in the shop. Images of victims' skins being used to make lampshades burned into me. I imagined myself as one of the unwired lamps: what it might have been like when it was first brought there, what kinds of expectations it had, which of the other lamps were once its friends, which ones had already been taken or thrown away. These thoughts kept flowing in me, and by the next rehearsal, I had already improvised many facets of the lamp's life, which then became the basis—the only real basis—for my successful character work in the play.

The same kinds of results can be achieved by working with animals. Any zoo will provide a feast of character ideas for you. A polar bear combines incredible power with lumbering grace. Which part of its body is the center of its power? Somewhere in its back? Try moving your arms or your legs from the lower part of your back. Get down on all fours and move around your room, with your lower back as the center of your locomotion. Raise and stretch your neck as if it was connected to your lower back. Growl like the bear; make the sound from as far down inside your body as you can, as if it too comes from your back. Think of the bear moving about in its surroundings as you walk about yours.

Maintain the back-centered movements, then slowly get to your feet. Standing upright, control everything you then do as a human being—

make a phone call, walk to the park, clean your room—with your lower back as the fulcrum. Practice using the movements and include attitudes that seem commensurate with these movements, like an unhurriedness about life. Like you can last a long time without immediate gratification. Like you have the confidence and the time to observe all kinds of life around you. If a threat of any kind arises, you know you'll be able to stand right up to it. So that in a very short while, you will have become bear-like. Then transfer the movements and the attitudes to your character's life.

Barbara Stanwyck credited the theatrical producer David Belasco with her authoritative, unhesitant walk. Belasco, she said, once remarked that women didn't know how to walk and advised her to learn by going to the zoo to watch the animals. She took his advice and ended up copying the stride of a panther.

Birds, reptiles, fish, even insects can set you going. I took over one of the two roles in Athol Fugard's *Blood Knot*. It had had a long run off-Broadway by the time I got into it. I was hired as an understudy just a few days before I had to go on—the actor playing the role had hurt himself badly. I'd hardly rehearsed, but the producer asked me to please try; I was young enough not to refuse. He gave me about six hours' notice.

I was very excited, of course, and then desperate. What was I going to use? What character traits, what attitudes, what kinds of physical behavior? (I also hoped I'd remember all the lines.) I thought over the part of Morris and began making a list of all the things described about him.

The play is set in South Africa. There are two brothers, one dark-skinned, the other (Morris) pale enough to pass for white (they had the same black mother but different fathers). Morris had left his black brother a year or more before the play begins, to find a place in the white man's world. Complicated feelings about his brother and the now-dead mother they shared make him return to the black township where they grew up. As a kind of penance, he now intends to care for his less-educated, disenfranchised brother.

I didn't want to copy my predecessor's performance (although there's nothing wrong with trying to duplicate a performance you admire—it's one of the ways to grow). I would certainly stick to all the staging I could, and the director's sense of the relationship between the brothers, but all the ups and downs of their new life together were to be mine, as were the fine details of Morris's individuality. Big dreams. Needed a lot more rehearsal time. But the evening's performance was on me, and choices had to be made.

I remembered that when I first saw the play, I was drawn by my character's openness and his great desire to please his brother. This immediately made me think of my own young son. When he was a baby, before he could talk, he made fetching mouth movements as he tried to follow things in which he was interested. Then I thought of Chaplin's Tramp, who, whenever he was in the position of being caught at something that might get him in trouble, would smile or laugh and shrug his shoulders as if to say "Who, me?" He would also try to endear himself to a potential antagonist in whatever ways he could. Those two ideas felt useful to me to help express Morris's new attempt at life with his brother.

But I needed something to help me relate actively to his recent past when he was off in the white world and lived in constant danger. If caught trying to pass himself off as white, he would have been beaten, imprisoned, and very possibly executed. He had to be ready to hide or run at the slightest hint of discovery.

An image jumped into my head that startled me; under any other circumstances, I can't imagine ever having thought of it. A cockroach. Caught unexpectedly when a light is suddenly thrown on at night, cockroaches will dash for cover. In one of my family's previous apartments in Manhattan, we were always on the lookout for those little beasties. They were a sign of filth, or corrosion, of invasion. They contaminated our kitchen in particular. We fought their intrusion with sprays, with traps, with any heavy object at hand.

I would sometimes go on nightly hunts to cut down their numbers, for in that apartment they usually emerged in hordes. And with what gleeful mayhem I greeted them! Late at night, I'd sneak into our kitchen as quietly as I could in my thick-soled work boots, switch on the wall light, and go to work—stamping, pounding, squashing all about me. It was always a slaughter.

But every once in a while, one of those miniature prehistoric creatures would scramble so madly, so wildly, in so many different directions at once, that I let it go out of perverse admiration of its will to survive. It was foolish of me, I suppose, since that little bugger would probably be the single best propagator of his entire roach family. But I have to admit that I admired its wild persistence, so I let it live.

And somehow I made a connection between that insect's instinct and my character, Morris. With the roach image in mind, I could visualize Morris in any number of situations outside his black township, instantly on the ready to rush out of danger's way, hoping that the intensity of his scrambling would provide him extra safety, or forgiveness.

I now had three solid choices to work with for the evening: the innocence of my infant son, the Tramp's need to endear himself to those about him, and the cockroach's manic physical alertness. They became the cornerstones, not only of my creative work in the play that night, but for the remainder of the run, which lasted another five months.

No actor ever knows ahead of time what he'll use to kindle his imagination toward his next role. Anthony Hopkins, a wonderful stage and film actor who has given us several memorably evil characterizations, recently created an especially demonic one in the film *The Silence of the Lambs*: Dr. Hannibal Lecter, otherwise known as Hannibal the Cannibal.

In speaking of his work on the part, Mr. Hopkins told the *New York Times*: "The most peculiar thing was the name: Lecter. Hannibal Lecter. The Lecter sound. It started like a clock in my brain. Lecter. And I saw a black box, like a black clock, something black or shiny, something veneered, a lacquered black killing machine."

Good actors always look for a spark, a key, a handle to connect them with their roles. Sometimes it comes in the shape of an an object, an animal, a painting, or even an impression. Sometimes it comes in the form of music.

Suppose you were working on a role that required you to be especially forceful, but not mean-spirited. A character who aspired to great accomplishments in life, but never wanted to lose or diminish her humanity; a character who could be deeply vulnerable, yet never feel small or insipid.

Just listen to the first movement of Beethoven's Fifth Symphony. Your character is all there in the music.

Suppose the part you were rehearsing needed to be saccharinely romantic, nonreasoning, flowing with soft, mushy feelings pretending to be deep and everlasting. Play Frank Sinatra's version of "Strangers in the Night."

Suppose you were cast as a warm-hearted, earthy young woman caught in a romantic relationship that becomes dangerous but exhilarating, and you almost lose your head as well as your heart. Listen to some of Vivaldi's Four Seasons; *you'll find all the notes you need.*

I'm not suggesting this use of music to put you in the mood. *That's another matter. That's for helping you induce feelings and emotions which you then shape toward your character. I am suggesting that instead of trying to push yourself into conventional reactions and behavior that you think might make you appear more forceful or earthy or mushy, you let the music guide you.*

Try to live up to the rhythms and the punctuations of the music in your own everyday behavior. Follow the long-line musical themes in the piece you've chosen and apply them to your own actions and attitudes. Get out of bed in the morning as the music dictates, and take your shower the same way. Soap yourself, scrub yourself in keeping with the music. Look for the spirit of the music (not the beat) and rinse yourself off to it. Prepare your breakfast with that music in mind. Carry it with you during the day and evening. Talk to friends. What kinds of food might that particular music encourage you to shop for? You probably wouldn't ask for Twinkies if your music was Bach's Goldberg Variations *(well, you might). Neither might you order steak. But you would probably shop for fresh baked bread, good cheese, fresh fruits or fresh vegetables. Your attitude toward life would turn purer, truer to your better instincts, and you'd stay with them for the long haul, not just for that morning or that day*

Working on a character is very individual, and sometimes not even rational. Late at night, trying to sleep, an actor will half-dream an image for the role, a way of behaving that clinches a missing link. A sudden thought can occur at any time that redirects the actor's search. During rehearsal, impulses can bubble up from somewhere deep in your unconscious.

Always remember that *you* are the hub of the wheel of creation. The spokes are what you search out and work on, but everything moves out from and returns to you, the center. Without a hub, there can be no wheel—not a wheel that moves.

The procedures and ideas I've suggested in this chapter are spurs to urge your creative mind. Some may provide methods by which you can actually construct a role, some are to help you fuse yourself and the character, and others, I hope, will be a stimulus to your own searchings.

When a young writer asked Ernest Hemingway how he ever made up all those stories and novels he'd become famous for, he replied: "I made them up out of everything I ever heard, read, saw, felt, or imagined happening."

How else do people create anything?

Text

In the early 1960s, John Gielgud brought his one-man Shakespearean compilation *The Ages of Man* to New York. In several pieces, he was extraordinary. He became an honored guest at the Actors Studio, and was given an adulatory introduction to us by Lee Strasberg.

In a shy, halting manner, Mr. Gielgud stepped before us. He straightaway begged off any speechmaking, and instead called for questions. The one that many of us wanted to ask came quickly: "How do you personally work on Shakespeare?"

"Ah yes," he smiled, hands pressed together in front of his chest, prayerfully. "That continues to be a lifetime question." He paused, searching for something true, something of value, then said, "You know, it's really all in the lines. When I have questions, and I always do, I go to the text. I place the words in my mind and follow them. It's always in there, somewhere."

The first acting school I attended was the Dramatic Workshop in New York City, then run by a genius of the theater, German-born Erwin Piscator. He didn't actually conduct classes himself when I was there, but I found myself assigned to two productions he directed.

Piscator used only students in his productions, and with three active theaters in production at all times, everyone who studied at the workshop gained invaluable stage experience. In the first production I helped gather props, then arranged them to be most convenient for the actors either going on stage or coming off. I was present, therefore, at all working rehearsals.

It was a production of *Romeo and Juliet* using mostly second-year students, and I was very impressed with the level of acting prowess of most of the cast. But Piscator had difficulty with one actor whom he accused often of being too literal. One day he stopped that actor in the middle of a scene and asked him what he was trying to say with a certain line that included the word "green." The actor, reacting defensively, said, "I thought the character was describing the color in order to..."

Piscator cut him off and heatedly said, "No darling, in this thought, it's not a color. It's greeeen." He stretched the word to emphasize what he meant, and used his hands to illustrate something coming to life. "Green," he repeated, almost conducting the vowel sounds in the word to give it the ripest sense of things growing. "Greeeen, you understand? Not about a color. About life."

The actor tried to mimic Piscator's voice pattern, but with none of the director's passion. Piscator repeated his example several times, the actor tried to copy him as exactly as he could, but always fell short. Here was a master director, renowned in Europe and the United States, trying to force a vision of life into the mind of a young actor who was already so stuck in his own linguistic habits that he was unable to adapt to any other.

Most of us were taught to read basic text by sentences: "Jane has a dog." "Dick has a cat." Two sentences with beginnings and endings. But both can be said as one thought on one breath to emphasize a connection between the two—as if there were an unspoken "but" in the middle, or as if you were appreciating Jane's dog while deprecating Dick's cat.

Human beings don't usually speak in formal sentences. Commas, semi-colons, colons, and periods are meant as approximations of various pauses and inflections we make while talking.

When we come to read a script, we bring along an accumulation of reading habits that serve literary purposes, not speaking ones. We also bring along other learned habits that interfere with the craft of translating the printed word into the language of human beings. The same is true for songs.

A four-line ditty like "Row, Row, Row Your Boat" can be hell on people who are guided only by punctuation or habit. Over many years, I have asked thousands of prospective actors wanting to study with me a few simple questions about the four lines in this song.

I begin by asking, "Do you know the words to 'Row, Row, Row Your Boat'?" The answer is mostly yes. I then say, "Okay.

Just run the words over in your head and tell me, *according to the lyrics*, how to row the boat and why."

Long pause as the students track the lyrics in their minds. Then I usually have to repeat the question: "How should I row the boat and why?"

The reply is either "gently" or "merrily," never "gently" *and* "merrily." The thought of rowing the boat gently and merrily does not seem to arise, because the punctuation and the phrasing separate the two adverbs.

Then comes the round-up question again: "Why row the boat?" About half the students are stuck, until I say, "It says why in the last line."

"Oh, right. Because life is but a dream."

Right. Now how come so much difficulty over so simple a text? Because as children in school, we were all taught this ditty in exactly the same way:

Row [pause]
Row [pause]
Row your boat [pause]
Gently down the stream [pause].

All those pauses helped our teachers gather us in groups, the second group joining the round on the word "gently," sometimes a third group on the word "merrily," and, if the class was large enough, a fourth group would chime in starting with "life." A wonderful device to organize children, have them all feel participatory—and regulated. (I remember sometimes actually being marched around the room to this song.) Just the opposite of what the words said. No teacher, or parent, ever gathered us together and pointed out the wonderful smiling attitude toward life explicit in these lyrics.

Here's another pointed misuse of text. What song has some of the horniest, sexiest words ever written? A classic ballad that was enormously popular in the 1940s and 1950s, still recorded and popular today—Cole Porter's "Night And Day." A crooner's and listener's delight, it's been in the movies and the title was used as a movie title as well. Yet what do its lyrics say?

Day and night, under the hide of me,
There's an oh such a hungry, yearning burning inside of me
And this torment won't be through
'Till you let me spend my life making love to you
Day and night, night and day.

These are the words of a sex-starved person. Do you think anyone has ever sung it that way? Heaven forfend. It's invariably
sung, by man or woman, as a soft-voiced, sentimentally romantic
piece with a full string section lushly featured in the orchestration.
Why? I suppose because it would be incredibly demanding on
any performer or listener to express or experience the full meaning of these words. Or possibly because at the time he wrote
them, Cole Porter himself knew he could only get away with
lyrics like these if he presented them in a warm, soupy orchestra-
tion. Who knows?

Is there a more terrible lyric to a children's song than "Rock-a-
Bye Baby"? Countless adoring parents have sung, "When the
bough breaks, the cradle will fall/And down will come baby, cradle and all." What a hellish message for an infant to hear from a
parent! The lyrics are couched in such a soothing, syrupy melody
that most parents don't realize what they are conveying.

Take the words of almost any successful jingle: "Things go better with Coke," "Pepsi-Cola hits the spot," whatever. No matter
how banal or unclear the words may be, with the right musical
arrangement, the jingle becomes part of our everyday life.

What we all know, but too often forget, is that almost everything we hear or read has been prearranged. A literary or musical
or vocal arrangement is repeated so often we become like
Pavlovian dogs in our conditioned responses to the arrangement,
not the words. From lullabies to commercial jingles the methodology is the same: take the most inadequate words, deliver them in
a saccharine or rousing way, and the recipient tends to remember
only the arrangement.

In years of coaching and teaching singers, I have never met
one who first sang what the words said, then worked on the
melodic interpretation. And the same is true for most actors.

Let's go back to "Row, Row, Row Your Boat." If the ending of the song is "Life is but a dream," *that* thought should infuse the earlier lines of the song, shouldn't it? So that the "Row row row your boat" phrase should have the same flow of thought and tonal feeling as the last line. Because that's what the words say. You are then free to interpret that basic idea any way you choose: you can be ironic about it, you can mock it, you can laugh at it. That's what interpretation means. But that's something you should *choose* to do, not just react your way into.

And the same goes for speech. Hamlet may begin his soliloquy with "O what a rogue and peasant slave am I," but he ends with "The play's the thing/Wherein I'll catch the conscience of the king." So clearly he's not passive here, he's in action from the beginning, looking for a solution. By the end of the speech he's found one. That's what the words say, and that quest for a solution can and should infuse the opening and middle lines of the soliloquy as well. You can then interpret that quest: you can have Hamlet challenge himself to find the solution, laugh at himself, tease himself, get drunk and hardly know what he's saying by the end of the speech. To interpret is your privilege. To define is craft.

It's universally accepted that dancers' practices at the barre are not to be mistaken for dance performances. The same is true for musicians; every instrument has exercises written for it, specifically to practice fingering or tone.

Actors are denied this privilege. Whenever one hears actors speaking words, it's the assumption of the listeners (as well as of the actors, usually) that the actors must immediately live up to those words or they're being irresponsible. There is no such thing as material written just for actors to practice upon.

So, for practical and artistic development, all actors should give themselves the right to use any written words with as much latitude in delivery as they can while exercising or rehearsing.

Lynn Fontanne and Alfred Lunt, one of the great acting couples of this century, found that by sitting facing one another and locking their knees together, they could drill their lines until all thoughts, feelings, and words melded into one organic piece that freed them imaginatively and emotionally. Then they could be separated by activities and behavior and still maintain their connection with each other, which they proved on stage time and again.

You should feel as free with the words of a Shakespeare monologue or sonnet as you would with the lyrics of any song that popped into your head while you were taking a shower. You should feel just as playful with any words you've memorized as you would if you were fooling around with a foreign dialect.

As a matter of fact, the more playful you can be with any written material as you rehearse, the sooner you will free yourself of one of the all-consuming fears of any actor: forgetting your lines in the middle of a performance. No matter how difficult memorizing lines can be, remember that no great actor was ever praised for how well he remembered his lines. That's not and never will be the issue.

In years of reading Shakespeare, acting his works, and seeing others perform his many roles, I was always struck by a line uttered at the opening of *Henry V* by the character called The Chorus. I've seen at least a dozen actors play this part in productions and scenes; I've also watched the two wonderful film versions, one directed by Laurence Olivier, the other by Kenneth Branagh. I have yet to hear one actor deal with this line as I believe it was intended to be read.

The Chorus is appealing to the audience, protesting that he has been given an almost impossible task by the playwright. He must not only introduce the circumstances surrounding a war between two great nations, England and France,   he must also find a way to engage the audience's collective imagination so that it will accept the image of two full armies waging battle on a small open-air stage hardly large enough for twenty or thirty actors. And the crucial lines Shakespeare has given him to express this dilemma begin:

O for a muse of fire that would ascend
The brightest heaven of invention:
A kingdom for a stage, princes to act
And monarchs to behold the swelling scene.

Finally, when a young actor in my class attempted to act this scene, I asked him if he knew what a muse of fire was. Was it listed somewhere? In Greek or Roman mythology perhaps? I said I'd read of muses of poetry, of love, and of dance, but I couldn't recall that one. And since he had spoken it with such assurance (as had every other actor I'd seen perform it), could he please tell us what sort of muse this fiery one was? The actor had no answer and neither did any of his classmates. I ventured to suppose that this might be the point Shakespeare was trying to make: that since the task he had given the Chorus was clearly impossible, perhaps there was some unknown muse—never before called upon—to help him in his travail. So that the line could very richly be said as someone *wishing* there were such a muse. Which would make perfect sense for the character in that situation. Here again, as in the musical arrangements of most lyrics, the rhythms of these Shakespearean lines as commonly taught (both here and in England), tend to make actors skim the surface of what's being said.

Dialogue presents a more complex way of looking at what words say because you have more than one person's thoughts and feelings being expressed at a time.

If you went to a party and a stranger came up to you as you entered and said, "You are so good-looking," then walked away, you might be pleased and intrigued. And if some ten minutes later, while you were piling some food on a plate, that stranger suddenly reappeared beside you and said, "But you probably eat too much," and vanished again, suspicion and annoyance might replace your previous pleasure. And if some few minutes later while you were engaged in conversation, the stranger came by again and said, "Please come with me, I need your help," you would probably think twice about going with this stranger. But whether you helped this person or you didn't, his words to you— all three remarks—would stay in your thoughts and your memory long after the event.

When two actors first engage in dialogue from a script, neither actor can remember the first three remarks of his partner two minutes after they are said. This has been my experience ninety-five percent of the time over the past thirty years, as I've watched countless scenes and plays being read.

I began to stop actors in a first reading after less than a full page of dialogue to ask what they were saying to each other. The results were almost always the same: each actor barely existed as a human being. Instead of communicating thoughts or attitudes about life to which his partner could then respond either negatively or positively, each actor had already decided on a reaction or a reading of his or her lines that sounded acceptable for the character that he or she was playing. I almost never found *two people* trying out what they were given to say by the author, attempting to perceive what their partner's reply could mean in terms of what had already been said.

In life, a human being enters a relationship by noticing the other person's attitudes toward many things in life. If the two agree with one another's major ideas and feelings about life, they usually become friends; if they are at odds over too many issues in life, they tend to avoid each other.

Shouldn't actors try to notice these similarities or differences in their characters? Certainly, we can sometimes be friends with someone we disagree with regularly—but usually only when a facet or quality of this person intrigues us, amuses us, or pleases us somehow. We tend to be aware of this quality and always keep it in mind. Actors, however, seem to blur over this awareness. Instead of using differences and/or similarities to vitalize relationships and accumulate thoughts and responses to use for their roles, most actors just move ahead to the next sequence of dialogue and try to get connected anew.

Remember, words mean nothing unless they convey ideas or feelings that can or should matter to those around them. Otherwise, why bother to speak? British actor Jeremy Irons put it this way in *American Film* magazine: "You think, you don't just speak. The lines come off the thoughts."

Early on in my training, I was introduced to the concept of *subtext*. Subtext includes the thoughts and ideas running through a character's mind underneath the written words. It seemed very sensible to accept the idea that no matter how valid a character's words appeared on the page, those words had to be only part of what the character might be saying or certainly thinking—just like in life. So each of us in class had to practice creating a subtext for any role we were working on. A monologue would be chosen, then our task was to write out another complete monologue that would represent what the character was *really* thinking while the author's monologue was being said.

Creating this other monologue was a fascinating and very valuable practice; it pushed all of us into a far more imaginative involvement with our roles. There was only one major flaw, which for a long time I was unaware of (or unable to define, or unwilling to argue about with my instructor). Try as I might—time after time, character after character, and even teacher after teacher—I found it impossible to stick to my sub-text. For every monologue's subtext that I wrote out and memorized, I would find extra, unexpected, unwritten, and unbidden thoughts. I didn't have the faintest idea of what to do with these thoughts (I actually considered the possibility that there might be something wrong with me for not being able to stick only to the thoughts and ideas I had proposed for my own use). It wasn't until years later that I realized it is just as impossible to regulate thoughts based on subtext as it is to base them on the author's words. Doing so is really another form of brainwashing.

There is no substitute for real thought in acting. Any effort to substitute made-up thoughts will cause glassy-eyed looks and tension throughout your system. Making up subtext is a helpful tool in exploring a character's inner life. But it can never, nor should it ever, be the final result of this exploration—unless it allows for *everything you actually think* while you're speaking.

In the book (and film) *Zorba the Greek*, a young Englishman, befriended and tutored by an old Greek named Zorba, is bewildered when the old man, who has had a series of personal and financial setbacks, suddenly gets an idea that may validate his life, and dances wildly. The Englishman expected laughter or words, but certainly not dancing. When he asks Zorba to explain, Zorba's reply is, "Sometimes a man feels so much all he can do is dance."

Which actually is an exercise I ask students to use to explore a scene. I tell them to dance it. Assume the attitude of a dancer or choreographer and make up movements that could clarify what happens in the scene, and the inner experiences the characters might go through. Even a short dance synopsis will help define the ideas and feelings in the written material.

When you've found appropriate movements, add sounds. Then try to maintain the vitality and intentions of these movements and sounds as you add the text back in.

Instead of dancing the material, you can sing it. There should be no judgment of your singing abilities. You don't even have to worry about appropriate melodies—you can make them up (just like the dance movements) depending on what you think about the scene and your responses to it.

In both these cases, you'll find yourself stretching out to the material, moving past the literalness you may be bringing to the words alone. You'll certainly gain in expressiveness and freedom of behavior.

By the time we formulate all the words necessary to express anything deeply, the force of the feelings involved has already lessened. Remind yourself of the difficulty of trying to convey your feelings and thoughts to a bereaved friend. We invariably end by hugging and crying along with them. Think of the incredible sounds of joy and relief that emanate from us when we face a badly hurt child who has miraculously survived. No words could possibly do as much.

In more frivolous circumstances, consider what might happen on a date if both parties decided to say anything and everything they felt or thought in sounds only from the first moment of greeting. The date might be over instantly. Or it might become a very intense relationship before the movie or the dinner even started. In any case, the couple would certainly know where they stood with one another in a very short period of time.

Babies express everything without words.

Somewhere, sometime, when my infant son gurgled and burbled noises at me, one of those gurglings was probably calling me, maybe even by name. However, I was unacquainted with his terminology, so I decided, like all decent parents, to get him to say the word "daddy." Then we'd both know what he was saying. And like all children, as his gurgling came closer and closer to the actual word, and my pleasure mounted, so did his. The more I burbled, "Good, that's it—Daaa-deee—good boy," the more he smiled and tried to get the sound right. Right for whom? Me. The adult. He'd been happily, freely, and naturally expressing his relationship to me in his noises. I forced him to articulate into my language. I'm not saying I was wrong; as adults, in society, we need common language. But my son's language was richer, more varied, and contained more intonations and feelings than mine did.

Now, as adults, we are all stuck with all these words, and must relearn how to infuse them with all the thoughts and feelings we are capable of.

Thoughts are clearly more difficult than feelings to put into sound and movement, but wonderfully worth the effort. In the early 1960s in the director's unit at the Actors Studio, after watching a scene from a very talky play, Strasberg asked an actor (who had just played the role of a mad scientist) if, when he said the line "This is it!," he was referring to the prop cannon on stage, or the town which was to be blown up by that cannon. The actor was puzzled. Strasberg then explained that he asked the question because when the actor had said that line, he had pointed his index finger at the sky, so Strasberg wondered what was up there. The actor's perplexity deepened. Strasberg suggested that "This is it!" could refer to the cannon, which was to be the means of destruction. Or perhaps, if the scientist pointed to the town, the gesture and the line could be taken as a warning to the inhabitants of that town.

The actor's eyes began to shift as his imaginative mind considered the alternatives. A marvelous mad gleam came into his eyes, and he suddenly used one hand to point to the cannon while the other hand snapped out toward the town. The words poured out in a triumphant "*This* is *it!*" He had included both! We all applauded.

If you cannot act out essentially what your words say in a given speech or dialogue *by using only sounds and movements*— no words at all—then you still have not come to understand what was written on the page.

Once you've learned your lines and had time to rehearse your material, another way of breaking through the literalness of text is to do what's called a speed-through, in which you say all the lines as quickly as you can while retaining the dynamics of the role. If you stumble, just use gibberish to continue the verbal pace until you can pick up the lines again.

It's amazing how many unexpected attitudes and impulses related to the scene will be released. (It's another sign of how much of what the material is really about has been going on in you unconsciously.)

John Gielgud must have realized the necessity of some of these things when he was fielding those questions at the Actors Studio. When an actor asked how often Mr. Gielgud found his answers in the text, he replied, "Ohh, about half the time."

Another questioner immediately called out, "Well, what do you do the rest of the time?"

Mr. Gielgud's face crinkled, he rubbed his hands together, and answered, "One slogs along as best one can, you know?"

That "slogging" means *you* have to get in there with those words, you have to try to convey what the character might (or might not) mean by them. You have to use *your* imagination, *your* wealth of experiences and observations, *your* vocal prowess, and *your* capacities for expression, to bring a role to life. The author has done only half the work—you have to do yours.

Auditioning

The purpose of an audition is to get you the job. Sometimes you'll get that job because you are eminently suitable for the role. Other times, it's because of what you can create for the role.

In the days of the famous Group Theater in New York, they had a special problem casting the lead for Clifford Odets' play *Golden Boy.* The Group Theater was, as its name implies, a group of actors working together over a period of years. All productions were cast from the members of the Group.

The title role in the play calls for a young violinist who becomes a money-making boxer to help support his family and his ambitious lifestyle. The only two members of the company considered even possible for the role were John Garfield and Luther Adler. As the directors discussed the qualities and capabilities of these two actors, their decision came down to the judgment that because Luther Adler was far more refined in his own persona than Garfield, the audience would readily accept his being a violinist—they could then teach him how to box. With Garfield, there was no question that he could act the fighter, but very few people would ever believe he could play the violin. Adler got the part.

Having sat on both sides of the casting table, I can tell you that more often than not, it isn't just the reading that gets the actor the role—it's the actor's qualities, plus the reading, that does.

Consider what those people on the other side of the room are looking for in an audition. First of all, you have to know that your auditioners want you to be good. I've never met a director or casting person who didn't hope the next person through their door would be perfect for the part.

Occasionally, after a good reading, the director will ask you to read again, and offer you an acting adjustment. Many times, that's really done to see if you can take direction; it may not have anything to do with the scene. Other times, the director may be looking for other qualities in your persona.

Stay open and flexible for your auditions, do your work as well as possible, and don't try to second-guess what's being looked for.

I remember an awful experience I had as a young professional reading for understudy for a very successful production of the play *Luv* on Broadway. The call said they were looking for someone to cover both Eli Wallach and Alan Arkin. I had seen the play earlier and thought both actors (as well as Anne Jackson) were marvelous. So was the direction.

When I came to read on stage, on the set of the play, I decided my main objective was to be as funny as the two actors I had seen, so I mimicked everything I could remember either of them doing. I was barely two minutes into the reading when a voice from the dark auditorium gently called out, "Mr. Miller, you've proved you can be funny, now would you please read the scene?"

It was the director Mike Nichols, whom I was trying so hard to impress. He was reminding me that first comes what the scene is about, later it can be made funny.

It always helps to know everything pertinent about your auditioners. If I had taken the time and trouble to research the kind of director Mike Nichols was, reminded myself of the kinds of work he had brought to earlier productions, or even what his performance style was as Elaine May's partner, I would have known better than to try to dazzle him with my comicality.

Even when you're just there for an interview, it helps to know some background on the people you've come to see. If it's a theater company, do they do experimental work or revivals? Have you seen a production of that company's recently?

If you don't know anything about your interviewer, be ready to improvise on whatever seems necessary.

After a couple of seasons playing substantial roles on television episodics produced at Universal, I was being considered for a lead role in one of their new series. As part of that process, I was summoned to The Tower—a big, black, monolithic office structure which houses most of Universal's top executives. One of these executives, whom I knew nothing about, was empowered with final casting approval over all talent in series.

I was nervous, but I'd focused hard on the character I was being considered for, was dressed appropriately, and was ready to demonstrate some of the attitudes and behavior I'd chosen for the part. Part of me felt confident about having gotten to this point.

On schedule, I was ushered into one of the corner offices with its magnificent view of the surrounding valley and mountains, and there was the gentleman in charge of my immediate future.

He smiled and greeted me; I smiled and greeted him. Then the conversation stopped. I waited for it to continue.

"Sit down," he said. I did, and suddenly realized that this was a relatively obligatory interview on his part, one that he was not particularly up for. My eyes flitted over the many objects on his desk and spotted a small baseball trophy.

"You play ball?" I asked, "Is that yours?" He lit up.

"Yeah. It's really for softball. I won it." He launched into a two-minute speech on how and why he received the trophy, and from there we went on to a fifteen-minute conversation about our own and others' softball exploits. It was very pleasant talk that not once addressed the topic of acting or the show I was being considered for, but I did get the part.

You don't need to waste valuable energy worrying if your auditioners are going to like you. Get in there, allow them their chatter, then show them your work.

If your audition is going badly, don't be afraid to stop and ask to start again. It would be foolish of you not to change direction if you were driving from Los Angeles to Montana and suddenly saw a sign saying "Dallas-Fort Worth Airport 2 Miles Ahead."

No one bats a thousand. The best hitters in baseball *don't* get on base over 60 percent of the time. No one, including you, can expect perfection, not in readings and not in performances. (Just a note: Native-American women in many tribes always make a deliberate flaw early on when weaving a blanket. They know perfection is impossible to keep living up to.)

Even if you've done your homework well, once you're in that audition room, the pressures can play havoc with your system. If you feel yourself functioning badly as you carry out your tasks, pause and remind yourself to breathe deeply, and do a quick relaxation. Either refocus on the acting choice you were on when you stopped, or think over what it might mean to you if you didn't pass the audition. Then let whatever opens up in you become part of your reading. Tension and/or lack of preparation are your two worst enemies.

If you are auditioning to become a member of an acting company or group, you have to think a little differently than if you are going for a single role. Your audition piece should then primarily demonstrate your versatility. Try to present as many facets and colors of yourself and as wide a range of emotion as you can within the context of your audition piece.

For instance, if you were to do an early soliloquy of Hamlet's, try to include some of the passion and unforgivingness that he heaps upon his mother in the later bed chamber scene. Let your auditioners see more of your capacities for the role than the one speech might allow. If you choose a scene for Ophelia, pick an early section of the text but drop in at least a hint of the vulnerability that leads this young woman to go mad and kill herself toward the end of the play. You will then have shown not only more of your range but also more of your perceptions as an actor.

It is, after all, an audition and not a performance. You are not given the entire piece to do for a reason. You are there to demonstrate your potential for many roles, not simply one.

The opposite is true when it's a specific role you are auditioning for. You then have to try to bring as much imagination and veracity to that particular part as you can. But you must also grow in some dimension as you present it: your character mustn't be nearly the same emotionally or psychologically when you finish the audition as he or she was at the beginning. And make strong choices, not ordinary ones. Even for a television or film audition.

Marlon Brando knew it was a long shot for him to be considered for the role of the Godfather in the film directed by Francis Ford Coppola. He was most known for playing quick-tempered rebels, men who were out for themselves and who were willing to muscle their way through life if necessary. The Godfather was a man who could guide his followers, who was looked up to for his wisdom, and who had strong convictions and beliefs—a warm family man who was ruthless only as a last resort.

Because he wanted that role badly, Brando asked for a screen test. For the test, he not only wadded cotton into his cheeks to help slur his speech and bring an immigrant's quality to his voice, but also stuffed cotton into his ears to keep from hearing the other actors lines. This forced him to mull over what might have been said, and made him concentrate intensely on the person speaking to him. It gave him an otherworldly demeanor, creating a man very careful in his considerations—a man who kept his own counsel and spoke only when he had reached a thoughtful decision.

No matter how natural or real the character seems to be, what you choose to do for the role has to be as out of the ordinary as you can make it. Anton Chekhov once said: "A dramatic story is not when a man gambles away his family's fortune then shoots himself, but rather when a man *wins* a fortune and then kills himself."

Look for a hidden dream or hope in your character and try to reveal it. Find idiosyncrasies of behavior and thought that can make your characters memorable even in their ordinariness. Surprise your auditioners.

I remember helping cast a play in New York. I had become an assistant to a well-known director, and usually read with the actors who were auditioning. The play had a lovely fairy-tale quality. In it was the role of a teenage virgin girl who falls in love with a teenage virgin boy, and against both their parents' wishes, they continue to see one another, until finally they marry themselves in the woods. They swear eternal love and devotion, and declare themselves married. A tough scene for anyone to carry off convincingly.

A young actress came in to read, dressed very simply in a nondescript skirt, peasant-style blouse, flat-heeled but polished shoes, white socks, and a beautiful flower in her braided black hair. She was unknown to any of us, but even on first sight there was something very fetching about her.

The director spoke gently to her. She replied quietly. And he asked her to read with me. Her head went down, she was clearly doing some kind of preparation, which took only a few moments, but when she looked up at me her face was already beginning to blush.

Talk about reactions! Within half a dozen lines, I was ready to marry her myself. The girl was magical. The color of her cheeks seemed about to burst through the skin, her eyes were pools of love and desire. She had memorized all her lines, but it took every iota of concentration I had to turn away from her to locate my character's lines.

Of course, she got the role—on the spot (except that we were still obligated to read a number of actresses). And she stayed just as magical in that scene when we rehearsed the play, and when it was eventually performed. It wasn't until the second week's rehearsal that the director was able to get her to confide to him what she was using to create that blushing transformation: *the image of a budding red rose growing out of each breast, a single white rose flowering from her vagina.* Knocked us out.

My very first acting job in Los Angeles came about through an interview with a television casting person. It wasn't supposed to be an audition, but it became one.

I'd moved to Los Angeles after twenty-odd years of earning my living as an actor in New York: doing a few parts on Broadway, a dozen or so Off-Broadway, forty or fifty summer stock jobs, twenty or more television roles, and seven different soap operas. I had reasonable expectations of a relatively warm welcome in Hollywood (according to all my actor friends who had moved out there earlier). But what I didn't have was an agent.

I discovered that without an agent there couldn't be much of a professional welcome of any kind, warm or otherwise. I looked. I tried. I had a videotape of what I considered excellent work to show, but no one seemed interested in viewing my New York acting. I hadn't yet paid my Hollywood dues.

Finally, I was able to secure the services of a personal manager who had known me in New York, who tried as mightily as he could to interest casting people on my behalf. It took months—almost five, to be exact. I found myself sweatily en route to an interview with Milt Hamerman, casting director at that time for "Kojak," a very successful television series at Universal Studios.

Mr. Hamerman was a wonder. He immediately perceived my anxieties. He understood what it was like to come from a recognized acting background and yet feel untried and unsure in this new Los Angeles environment. Milt was from New York himself, and still spoke with a trace of that city's unmistakable vowel and consonant sounds. He was a large, genial man who, within a few minutes, helped me feel like a human being, not an actor trying to maintain his cool. I was talking. I was laughing. I was having an unexpectedly okay time with a top casting executive at one of the major studios. This was good.

But suddenly a series of thoughts popped into my brain, right in the middle of something he was saying, almost exactly like one of those light bulbs going off in a cartoon character's head: What am I doing? How is this nice, friendly disposition I've gotten into going to help me land a part on "Kojak"? They don't use guys like that. They use cops and bad guys, gangsters, hoodlums, connivers. Well, he's already seen I can be straight, a nice-guy kind of cop, maybe a shopkeeper or a lawyer. But all the really good parts on that show are the bad guys.

Thoughts fly quickly. Milt was still in mid-sentence as I unflexed my mouth, tilted my head, slouched slightly in my chair, stretched out my legs, breathed heavily and interrupted him in a guttural, street-tough voice that came from my younger days living in a gang-structured section of Brooklyn.

I told him he was a real slime who gathered his power from interviews like mine, where the guy coming in had no defenses, no position. I called attention to how fat he'd gotten sitting behind that big desk doling out benevolences like a big city potentate. His eyes got very wide. He stopped speaking. He looked as if he might almost have stopped breathing.

I cursed him, using every street-strewn obscenity I could quickly think of. I gathered my body and coiled up out of my seat and leaned over his desk, my voice getting very loud and very threatening. He stared at me, unbelieving, as I crescendoed into one last giant curse at him, and slammed my fist down on the desk, inches from his face. He jumped back in his chair and held there. I stopped, straightened up (still breathing pretty heavily), sighed deeply, and shrugged my shoulders and arms, as if to say sorry, but I had to do that.

Milt will always have my gratitude for the grace with which he accepted my performance. It took him several moments to fully recover, but when he did, he said, "That was very impressive."

I started to apologize, but he waved me quiet, smiled a little, and said to sit down. I did. He stared at me, mulling me over, then looked down at a script at the side of his desk, and said, "You know, there's a part in this week's script..."

I couldn't restrain myself. "You mean it? There's really...?"

He stopped me again. "No, no, no, no. It's a long shot, it's just a thought. But I wouldn't even have thought of it if you hadn't done that. Let me think some more about it. I'll tell you this, you're going to work on this show before the season's over, I promise you. Now go home and let me think about it."

I did get the part. And it was quite a good one: a punch-out hit man who was featured all the way through the script. But until that day in that office, I had never played such a man in my entire acting life.

It was a daring thing to do, and it easily could have backfired, yet my desperation and a good deal of acting skill helped it pay off.

I don't advocate attacking casting people, but I do advocate coming to an audition, or even an interview, prepared to demonstrate your versatility.   If you need glasses to see with, find some excuse during an interview to remove them. Look for an imaginary dust speck to clean off, or an eyelash that seems to have nearly gotten into your eye.

If you've been sitting very quietly for a while, make sure you suddenly shift your body forward or stand to demonstrate you're not locked into one behavior.

If you've been talking quietly, raise the intensity of your voice every so often. If you've been on one pitch, change to a lower or higher one. If you've chuckled a few times, make sure you give at least one full-bodied laugh.

If your reading of the role has been in one mode, say, considerate and moderate, try to include a trace of aggressiveness or cynicism.

Don't shy away from shifts in your character. Look for facets that *could* be there: a shy character can be confident in certain areas, a persuasive lawyer can forget what he or she is saying for a moment.

Never count on a casting person or director or producer or even your agent knowing what you are capable of acting—you have to show them.

Don't worry about behaving differently for a film audition than for a stage audition. Walter Brennan, the wonderful movie character actor who began his career on stage, put it succinctly many years ago in an interview. Asked about the difference between film and stage, he explained: "In film, if it's a long shot you act it big, on a medium shot, medium, and on a close-up, in the eyes. But you always act *it.*"

The same is true for your audition. If it's in an office, you act whatever you've chosen to act within the parameters of that space. Which doesn't mean you have to be quiet and careful. On the contrary, you should be emotionally vivid but physically controlled—you don't need your entire body to express yourself. If they put you on a stage or out in large room, then use all of yourself largely.

As a practical matter, even if your audition takes place in a small area, I would urge you first to act out whatever you're going to bring in as big as you can. You can always make your choices more subtle, but it is very difficult to reverse the process. I would urge you to do the same when you actually have the part. Try everything big first. If your character keeps a lid on, you have to be able to express what's under that lid, don't you? So which do you work on first? Obviously, what's under the lid.

For every stage of acting—audition, rehearsal, and performance—you want to be in as creative a state as possible. But there is no way simply to *be* creative; you have to *do* something creative, and all creative work for an actor includes using your imagination. Actors never use only what is real: the blood you spill on stage when stabbed is from capsules, the brother you betray in a film is not your real brother, the boat you drown in floats in a tank of water only three feet deep. Creating the illusion of reality is the actor's real world. The sooner you use your imaginative powers to help you act, the better.

It's a very interesting thing, this aspect of human behavior called imagination. In our everyday lives, we have to deal with practical and necessary matters like getting to work, paying bills, shopping, making and answering phone calls. They all seem to require only being sensible and logical. Yet people are capable of varying the details of these activities in all kinds of ways so that doing them feels less mundane.

People who ride the bus usually bring along reading matter to entertain their minds. Those who drive listen to the radio. Most of us fuss over which check designs to order for paying our bills; we want those checks to reflect something in us that's a little out of the ordinary. Grocery shopping includes not just purchasing necessities but choosing treats for ourselves as well as for friends who may drop by—foods that speak for our attitudes towards life. Almost everyone I know with a telephone answering machine tries to leave a fresh, individual-sounding message for callers, and when talking to an answering machine, many of us become more fanciful than when talking to a person.

I've seen people hose their lawns to musical rhythms, decorate their cars with Van Gogh-like paintings, make mailboxes in the form of a Swiss chalet, dress their dogs like showgirls. There's no end to mankind's imagination in short spurts.

But for acting, we need our imagination to flourish for long and sustained periods, not just to fill up time or to entertain friends or to show off. We need to be able to cultivate our imaginative resources in regular and sustainable ways.

When, in most of our usual lives, are we able to do that? When we read a book or watch a film or a play, we are able to do it.

I'm sure you've all had the experience of getting into a really good book that has you turning pages well into the night. Often it's a book of some three hundred pages or more, probably nowhere close to your own life even if it's nonfiction, and yet it can consume your imaginative attention for hours on end. If you have to leave it to go to the bathroom or to answer the phone, you don't have to reread several pages to pick up the thread of the writing. You can usually read on from precisely where you left off.

Which means that your imaginative, empathic responses have not really stopped or evaporated while you were away, they were merely put on hold.

The same is true when you see a movie or a play. You can leave your seat or change it, you can dash out to the lobby for refreshments or to make a forgotten phone call, and still, when you return, you can pick up the thread of your involvement without a sense of emotional interruption. A theater audience is capable of sustaining its imaginative involvement for at least two hours or longer. (If you find a double-feature movie house, we're talking about four to six hours some of the time.)

What allows us to do that?

To me, there are three basic elements at work. One is that our actions in all these cases are voluntary. We choose to read the book or pay to sit in the theater; no one is forcing us. Two is that we allow ourselves the liberty of familiar and comforting objects near us: when reading, we plump ourselves down on our sofas or beds or in chairs that support us cozily, we arrange the lighting so it's congenial, we either keep munchies alongside us or we make sure the refrigerator is stocked. In a theater, we look for seats without springs that attack us, and we arm ourselves with popcorn or chocolates or soda or gum. The third essential element is that we are free to leave our seat or our book at anytime for any reason.

I mean, imagine if you were sitting in a movie theater watching *Lawrence of Arabia,* and halfway into the film the theater itself became as blazingly hot as the desert on the screen, and sand suddenly began filling up the space around you. Imagination be damned, this is too real, you'd think, and you'd run for the exit.

We need to maintain a little distance between ourselves and the subjects we want to empathize with in order to have our imaginations stirred. We need to know we've chosen to enter these fictional worlds. We need to keep certain familiarities of our own regularly available. And we need to know we can leave the material at our own discretion.

On your way to an audition, try to slip in and out of the material you're performing, to establish that it's your choice. Behave like the character while you're dressing, then switch back to your own habits. Go back and forth several times. Talk like yourself if you answer the phone, then move into your character's vocal qualities and attitudes. Mull over the character's dilemmas, then relate back to your own. Make it clear to yourself that it's always you behaving, but that sometimes you *choose* to be more like her or him.

Then you'll need familiar things to surround yourself with at the audition itself. Laurence Olivier used to call these things his "green umbrellas." For a role in a Restoration play, he felt stuck with his inventiveness until one day, culling through the props department of the theater, he spied a green umbrella, which so reminded him of someone in his own life who behaved like the role that he immediately felt the relief of familiarity, and used the umbrella to play the part. Forever after, he always looked for other "green umbrellas" to help him into his roles.

The great Stanislavski was forever placing objects from his own family members' lives in hiding places all about the stage or in his pockets when working on parts—objects like lockets, rings, letters, pieces of embroidery. He knew that every once in a while, he would need contact with these objects and images of his own to stay empathic with his characters.

I've sometimes gone further. When doing a scene with an actor I had difficultly relating to, I resorted to writing notes (funny or nasty) about him, notes which I stuck underneath or behind furniture he sat on or used—without his knowledge, of course. It was very comforting, as well as stimulating, to think about my hidden notes while addressing him during our scenes.

One truly basic dilemma of unfamiliarity for all of us in an audition comes from the audition space itself. Whether it's an office or a rented hall, the space is invariably the producer's or the casting agent's. Nothing in it is ours.

No one functions very well in a totally foreign environment. Of course, you can pretend to know where you are and how to behave—which is what most of us do in such a situation. Yet no amount of handshakes or personal chatter really makes much creative difference. You are there to bring life to a fictional character, not to discourse on home mortgages or an article in

Variety. You need to find turf conducive to your imagination.
Here's a technique for accomplishing that. I call it *visualizing a place.*

Pick a subject or title to help you choose a place: luxury, leisure, business, service, family, a place you felt free to be alone in, a place you were never alone in, a place suggestive of friendship, betrayal, mischievousness. The place should have been familiar to you from at least five years ago; use nothing within the last five, unless your experiences in it began earlier than that period. It's whatever locale pops into your mind when you present yourself with the subject. It doesn't actually have to have been luxurious, for example, it just may have appeared that way to you.

The aim is not to try to arouse any particular feelings from this place, so if you find yourself resisting the subject or seem to be unable to choose one, look for its opposite. Instead of luxury, pick a place suggestive of poverty; instead of friendship, look for a place of alienation. The idea is to give yourself a starting point.

When the place has been selected, seat yourself in any chair that's handy, and think of being seated somewhere in that place. If it's a room, you might imagine yourself against the wall, or right out in the middle. Your position doesn't matter; whatever occurs to you is fine.

With your eyes open, and always with easy breathing and in a relaxed state, begin to visualize what would be directly in front of you if you were in that room. Not what feelings you may have had in this room, only what your eyes would have seen: how far the wall opposite you would have been. How high above you was the ceiling. How far to your right was the door. How far from the door was the armchair. And so on.

You will see the real furnishings of the space you are seated in, but let your eyes move past and around them. Don't make believe they're not there. You're constructing the imaginary room around them. You are not trying to be in that imaginary room. You are not trying to remember smells or sounds. You are not trying to recreate any incidents, or even any people. If such memories flit into your mind, usher them out gently, don't force them out. Accept their presence but continue to waft them on their way.

Also, try not to jump your focus from one part of the room to anoth-

er: move your eyes evenly from a wall to a chair or across the floor to any of the furniture. If you'd like to change your focus from one part of the room to another, or just take a breather, close your eyes, turn your head and/or body, then reopen your eyes and continue, but always let the details of the room accumulate.

Now comes the tricky part. After a while, four or five minutes at least, get up from your chair and take a slow easy walk around whatever actual space you are in. Move the room around with you. Keep the same proximity to the walls and furnishings as you had when you were seated. Whatever was in front of you should stay in front of you. Go slowly. You will lose some of the visual details as you walk (that's fine—I never said you ever had to see the room). Just allow yourself the leeway of its presence ebbing and flowing.

As you walk about, keep visualizing the details of your place around the objects and furniture and walls of the room you are actually in. Use your will power. Stick to your place's physical structure.

After a short walk, settle down away from the chair you originally sat in, and reconstruct your chosen place from your new position. Now begin to include some of the actual objects in the real room as part of your imaginary place. No need to motivate their presence, just include them. Then leave them out. Alternate the procedure.

You'll soon find that the imaginary objects help you see the real ones more freshly. And as you focus your sight from the actual furniture and objects to the visualized ones, a real creative sense begins to operate. You will feel you are doing something mysteriously engaging, real but unreal, private and personal. No one else can do what you are doing because no one else is privy to the place you are imagining. And you have complete power over its presence—or absence. (It's a taste of what the great British actor Ralph Richardson meant when he said, "Acting is like being in a dream.")

Practice with any place for a few days. Take your place with you to your bank. Begin to visualize it as you stand in line. Bring it forward as you greet your teller, and while he or she is busy with your paperwork, visualize your place around him or her.

Try it at your hairdresser's. Or the dry cleaner's. Give it an opportunity when you're stuck in bumper-to-bumper traffic. Or on a bus. Or at a friend's house. Be really daring and try it on a date.

When it truly feels yours to do with as you please, bring it with you to an audition. Use it in the waiting room, and carry it with you when you are called in to greet your auditioners. Then, suddenly and through an act of imagination on your part, they will be in your space, if you want them to be. Or you can keep them out of your place if it seems more propitious; it's yours, not theirs. And they will never know you had that power over them the entire time you were with them. What a wonderful feeling for an actor to have in an audition.

And what a graceful way to practice some of your craft.

Back in New York, a friend of mine who was basically a stand-up comedian at the time was called in for a comic character in Shakespeare's *Two Gentlemen of Verona*. It wasn't to be a reading—the people in charge had seen him perform as a comic—but they wanted to get a sense of him in person.

He also found out they were expecting him to be improvisationally amusing in the office. "You know," he said to me, "they're gonna want to see if I can be funny on the spot. Help."

I asked him who or what amused him. He mentioned a few comedians—and an uncle. I asked him to describe the uncle. But it turned out it was really how many jokes the uncle knew. Then he remembered his dog. He seemed to know every detail of that creature from the crevices in its ears to the size of its paws. He smiled endlessly while describing the dog to me.

I offered him a challenge: "Either take the dog with you to the interview, or *imagine* he's there with you and after a while he'll need to go relieve himself. Only your auditioners should never know what you're imagining."

He loved the idea, and he used it. He told me later he'd had a marvelous time thinking of his invisible dog, and was smiling and funny all through his interview.

He got the role. (And during rehearsals, which were in the open air, he befriended a stray dog that followed him everywhere and eventually became part of the production. See how life does imitate art?)

There comes a time in everyone's life when the lessons and experiences of the past seem unequal to the task at hand.

Circumstances suddenly present us with a difficulty we feel unprepared for.

That's how I actually passed my first audition for the Actors Studio. When an actress friend of mine signed up to audition for the Studio, still in its heyday in 1953, I had no desire to audition with her. I was happy studying with Uta Hagen and believed the Studio was too insular and precious about itself. The signs were against my going there.

However, financial circumstances intervened. I was suddenly no longer able to afford Uta's classes, and unfortunately no scholarship was proffered. The Studio, if you became a member, was free. Plus my friend's partner had backed out on her, and since a place on the audition schedule for the Studio wouldn't come again for months, I reluctantly agreed to help her.

She had already picked the scene: the opening of Jan De Hartog's *The Four Poster*, which had been a tour-de-force vehicle for Jessica Tandy and Hume Cronyn on Broadway. It chronicles a couple from their early marriage to their old age.

We rehearsed hard and long, the specialness of the audition beginning to press in on us both. It began to feel as if all our acting eggs were now to be in this one audition basket for the foreseeable future.

The evening of the audition we arrived early, but so had the twenty or thirty acting pairs who preceded us. The tension and the sweat in the waiting room increased greatly when it was announced that any scene longer than five minutes would be cut off at that point. Ours was about eight.

Our wait was over two hours long. Our personal preparations for the scene had come and gone at least a dozen times. By the time we were called, I would gladly have disappeared and disavowed any intention of ever trying to act again in my life. But my friend's eyes said "please."

I marched with her to the open door of the audition room. It was very dark on the other side except for one area of light. I picked my partner up in my arms (which is how the play actually opens, with the groom carrying his bride over a threshold), and headed for the light. As I reached the area, my heart thumping, perspiration gluing my shirt, jacket, and skin into a single mass, I took a deep breath, tried in vain to regulate my nervous system to be able to speak, when—my knees buckled and I literally dropped my partner on the concrete floor.

I thought I might have broken her back. I was stupefied. She murmured from the floor. I stood helplessly. She said her first line. I didn't know what to do. She said her second line. I kneeled beside her uttering my line, but with my eyes locked on hers, looking for the slightest hint of pain or anguish. She kept going. So did I. I really didn't know what else to do.

She soon disengaged herself from the floor, checking for any dislocations of bone or dress. I hovered as the friend I actually was, tenderly and apologetically, until it was very, very clear that she was hurt in no way other than her feelings. The smiles of relief radiated out of me. Our kisses were entirely meant.

We finished the scene and wandered arm-in-arm to the exit, only once looking back at our hidden-in-the-dark auditioners, but not really caring at that moment whether we had passed our audition or not. We were both too happy that my partner was alive.

But pass we did. Because on that occasion, as we learned later, our auditioners were looking for our potentials, not how well we did the scene.

I've already described one audition Barbra Streisand passed for the lead role in *Funny Girl*, and mentioned that she had to audition twice more before she actually got the part. After convincing the producer and director that she had the requisite maturity to play Fanny Brice, her fifth and sixth auditions were to demonstrate her emotional range and ability to maintain emotions without becoming shrill or forced.

We worked hard to accomplish those results, and we both felt that she had more than satisfied their requirements. She had gone through six auditions—far more than anyone else they were considering. She had run a gamut of comedic and dramatic acting, but they were demanding one final audition from her. That's the way it was put to her: one last look at everything she could put together in a monologue of the character's, and they promised that would determine their decision. What a load to drop on a young actress.

We sat together in her apartment the night before the audition, going back over all the procedures, images, and tasks she had used previously. We restirred them, and she got emotional, and she was funny, and she was moving, and she became young and mature, equally. I thought she was in great shape. But by the end of the evening, I could see that she was not so sure. I tried to plumb her doubts, but they were not accessible. She turned very quiet and insular.

I watched her silently for a few moments until she looked me in the eyes, and then I said, "I want you to promise me something."

"What?" she replied, sounding like she really didn't want to know.

"Tomorrow, when you get there, if you begin to doubt any of these things you've worked on, if you begin to feel they're not right or not enough, or if you feel like you're not up to doing them that morning—I want you to promise me that you'll stand still, breathe deeply, relax, and ask yourself what it means to you *not* to get this part. Then open your eyes and start the monologue."

She stared at me, tears welling up in her eyes. Slowly, very still, she nodded slightly and said, "I promise."

"Then go to sleep," I said, and left.

The next day, an hour and a half after her scheduled audition time, her manager, Marty Erlichman, called me.

"She got it," he said. "But it was amazing what she did."

I was elated. "Tell me."

"She got there late..."

"I knew she would."

"...Robbins [Jerome Robbins, the director] was furious. He really yelled at her: 'Forty minutes we've been sitting here waiting for you—now you better be worth it.'"

"Wow."

"That hurt her, I could see it. I mean, he had a right to be mad. I thought for a minute that she was going to yell back at him or just stalk on out, but she just stood there. She got this very determined look on her face, then she let out this big sigh and closed her eyes. I didn't know what she was doing. She stood absolutely still, just breathing and sighing for a few seconds, or a minute, I don't know. All of a sudden, this smile came on her face, she opened her eyes, and she was all emotional—not just crying or anything, but all lit up. Then she started talking, and I tell you, she took the roof off. She was incredible. When she finished, Robbins jumped up and he was yelling at her, laughing and hooting 'That was great. As far as I'm concerned, you're Fanny Brice.' He hugged her, and everybody else was applauding and yelling great things at her. She was fabulous. What was she doing?"

I explained what we had gone over the night before. Marty accepted what I said, but he admitted that he couldn't account for the way it had all worked.

It's not that logical, Marty. Only actors, and some directors, are usually privy to the creative process of acting. It's a wonder wheel of mixtures—not like the wheel of chance in a casino where you pays your money and you takes your chances, but a wheel of invention and imaginativeness.

The hub is always you. The spokes are objects, images, tasks. We move out from our hubs, we actors, we travel out and among the spokes we have chosen to surround ourselves with. We move out, and move back, move out and move back, and the wheel begins to move. The more openly and fully we move out and back, the more movements the wheel is capable of making. Endlessly. Tirelessly.

It can be done. Even in an audition.

Rehearsals

Once you have the job, rehearsals begin. I'm going to separate what I say about rehearsals for television and film from those for a play, because they're two entirely different work situations.

In television, there is even a huge disparity between the way a sitcom is rehearsed and the way an episodic is done. "Sitcom" is short for situation comedy—which is half an hour long, usually shot with three or four cameras on videotape, sometimes in front of a live audience, after rehearsing for three or four days. An episodic television show is an hour-long, one-camera production that is filmed over seven to nine days.

In the sitcom world, the first day's order of business is a cast reading for the producers (who are usually also the writers) and the director. After reading, the cast is dismissed so the writers can haggle over what works and what doesn't. If the script is in decent shape, the actors are called back later the same day to begin rehearsing; if not, they wait until the second day while the writers rewrite. Changes are given and the director is left with the actors to put everything on its feet, which means blocking out behavior and activities for the characters. Unless there is some special effect required that needs to be rehearsed separately, the script is dealt with chronologically.

One or two days are spent blocking, without cameras, but with regular supervisory visits from the writers and/or producers. Additional script changes can and do take place during this period. Then comes blocking with the cameras, synchronizing the rehearsed behavior and activities with the camera operations, and the director deciding on which shots to use.

Next, the show is dress-rehearsed in sequence. Further changes in the script often take place after this go-through as the powers-that-be try to fix any continuing weaknesses in the script. If the changes are large, they're rehearsed and re-dressed. If not, they're given in the form of notes and put into practice the following day, in the first of two performances before an audience. The audience is usually warmed up by a hired comedian, sometimes abetted by one or more of the stars of the show. The cast is introduced to wild applause, and the first show is taped.

A dinner break is taken, more notes given, and the second taping is done a couple of hours later. If there are any bloopers or major bungles during this taping, they're either re-shot immediately or directly after the performance. Studio audiences are sometimes kept for hours after the second show to repeat their laughs and applause at appropriate moments.

That's sitcom life. For the actors, there's not too much discussion of the ideas in the piece or character relationships. There is a great deal of joke-fixing, plus tinkering with lines and activities.

Episodics (hour-long television series) and films share several things in common: they're almost never taped, they never use a live audience (unless it's part of the action), and they're almost always shot out of sequence.

If you're one of the regular players on a TV series (or one of the stars in a film), you are usually allowed some input as to how your character is written. You're also allowed to suggest line changes, and this applies if you're a guest star as well.

But as for rehearsals, if you're not a star, everyone—regulars, guests, and day players—is in the same boat. If you want to rehearse, you have to get together with your fellow actors off the set, usually in one of your dressing rooms, to run over the lines and try to discern any possibilities of relationship or dynamics in your scenes, which will run in length from twenty seconds to two minutes. When you're called by one of the assistant directors to "rehearse" on the set, all you'll be given by the director is blocking and a chance to run over the lines again.

Each time you're called to the set to rehearse, it's very much like auditioning: you never know ahead what the director may want, you have to arm yourself with strong and variable acting choices for your role, come out of your trailer/cubicle as confidently as you can, and do your best in this unknowing state.

Once in a grand while, a director—invariably one who started as an actor or stage director—will take the time to talk over your scenes and encourage your input. It still won't be for very long. Then off you'll go for a couple of rehearsals with the camera.

Finally, the director will call for a "take."

The camera will now roll. If all goes reasonably well with the camera, lighting, and sound, and your performance is adequate, that's the only time you'll do the scene. Rule of thumb for film is at least two takes per sequence, unless it's a dangerous stunt, which will be done only once if possible. If it's an important film, i.e. producers of status, a respected director, well-known stars, and a script by a notable writer—there could be many takes.

From 1975, when I moved to Los Angeles, until the end of 1991, I had acted in approximately two hundred television shows, pilots, films made for television, and features. From the beginning, I was given billing as at least starring, guest starring, co-starring, or also starring, and many of the shows I did were as a series regular. During that entire time, doing all those shows, I was given real rehearsals only eight times. And four of those occasions were on different "Barney Miller" episodes.

"Barney Miller" was the only show in my experience on which the guest stars were encouraged to bring in any interpretation they had for their roles. Time would be taken to try out those interpretations; scenes would be discussed, rehearsed, then taped. Everyone involved would gather about the TV monitors and look the scenes over. More discussion and possibilities were raised, rehearsed, and taped again. The show became infamous for its final tape-day schedule. We would all often stagger home at 5:00 A.M.—but staggering or not, we felt engaged in a creative process.

Of course, the stars of any piece can ask for more extensive rehearsals, but actors who don't have that kind of position or power can't.

You regularly get full rehearsals only when you work on a play. Minimum time to get a full-length play on the boards is a week, which is really only the case in summer stock. By the time the play has reached stock, it's already been produced elsewhere and all the stage directions and activities (called "business") are in a published version of the material. Even in this limited time for a stock production, you are at least working chronologically with your material, and there is some opportunity to discuss and evaluate your work.

A more usual rehearsal period for a play is three to five weeks, working six days a week, eight hours a day. During this period, there's a good deal of time to discuss and discover what your character and the play seem to be about. But whether in stock or on Broadway, until you hit your first audiences, neither you nor the best of directors really knows what works.

So the responsibility for creating your role on stage, on film, or on television rests mainly with yourself. Some of the techniques I'm going to suggest will appear to relate more to stage rehearsals than those for TV or film, but the principles are the same for every medium.

Your very first order of business is to relax and read your script. Take a few minutes. Get yourself in the same frame of mind and body as when you're settling down to read a new book. Then read your script exactly the same way, with as open a mind as possible.

When you're finished, ask yourself: What is it about? Not the plot, the theme. The theme of the piece is the idea behind it. The plot is the story, such as: Against his and her father's wishes, a conquering warrior falls in love with, and marries, a young, ethnically-different woman. The warrior is then tricked by his best friend into believing that his new bride has cuckolded him, and he kills her.

That's the basic plot of Shakespeare's Othello—*but that's not the theme.*

In this play, the theme could be: Without trust, love is doomed. Or it might be a question: What makes goodness succumb to evil?

The theme is what should drive you on as an actor in the piece. The author has already written the plot. Audiences will get that part no matter what you do. Your task is to help make them feel and think about what's at stake in the plot.

Some plays or films give you a thematic idea in their titles, like Long Day's Journey into Night. *With that one, you know you and your audience are going to be in for a deep, possibly anguished, very intricate, soul-searching time.* Summer and Smoke *can remind you of a fullness of growth and ripeness (summer), and hopes and dreams that sometimes go up in smoke. Even the title of a light farce like a* A Flea in His Ear *can suggest that the slightest rumor can change someone's life.*

The theme is there to set your imagination to work, not to give you an answer. It's there to help guide your adventures with the characters and the material into whichever choices of attitude and behavior best help maintain the theme.

So write out a theme for any piece you're working on, even if it's only a scene or monologue. Put it down and think about it as if it's the title of an essay you're about to write—just like we all had to do in school. You know, when the teacher would say, "Now I want you to write five hundred words on the subject of...." And the subject or theme could be anything: your favorite vacation, the causes of the American Revolution, whatever.

It's going to be your choice of subject. Let yourself go with it. Let it take you wherever it wants to, and get involved with its possibilities.

Suppose your theme is Love Conquers All. Start warming yourself to this idea: remember incidents you've lived through, stories you've heard, books you've read, films you've seen, and music that captures this theme. Even articles in the newspaper—perhaps one about an adopted child and its natural mother who find each other after years apart, or a group of Vietnam veterans who treat Vietnamese soldiers to a reunion.

Try to empathize with that child or mother, or any of those soldiers. Let your imagination fill in details of their lives apart, then try to act out how they might have felt and behaved during their meetings.

If it's an incident from your own life, give yourself time to dwell on the kind of person you were before the incident took place: what interests you had, whom you spent time with, the kinds of activities you pursued, then how this incident may have changed your prior behavior and feelings.

If you use a book or film, go over all the details you can remember of what was written or shown about the characters before, during, and after the theme is revealed.

Find a piece of music that embodies your theme. Don't just listen to it, get your body involved, let different parts of you join the orchestra-tion. Never mind the rhythm. Move your head and neck as if they were the instruments in the orchestra playing, then let your shoulders and upper back take over, then your arms, your lower back and hips, and so on. (This is also a great warm-up exercise for all occasions, in or out of rehearsals. You can even include smaller sections of muscles at a time, such as in your nose or lips, to join with the instruments.)

Whichever sources you use to flesh out your thematic statement, let the images and feelings they arouse seep into your thoughts and behavior as you deal with your daily life.

Every once in a while, look for opposites. What idea would be contrary to the one you've chosen? Again, if it's Love Conquers All, an opposite thematic idea might be Life Is Nothing But Betrayals (you'll find plenty of material to support that credo). Look for those incidents that move you consistently, especially from long ago. I still remember how devastated I was at the age of eleven when my mother, without telling me, put my pet cat to sleep because the cat was always getting pregnant. Whenever I summon up the images of that cat and all the private times I spent communing with her, I am filled with confounding emotions.

Use your thematic and contrathematic images often. Bring them to rehearsals. Have them hover around you. They may not give you answers for your role, but they will always provide you with a persuasive base from which to explore. And just as in any form of exploration, the further away from home base you go, the more likely you are to get lost. Stay in touch with that base and your explorations can become limitless.

Once you've warmed yourself toward the theme, ask yourself how your character relates to it: does he or she support it or resist it? Does he or she help others to it, or is the character concerned with it only for his or her own sake?

Travel the whole length of the script, not just any one scene your character may be in. Try to perceive what physical actions, impulses, feelings, and words the character uses to support or encourage his or her position, and which of the other characters either hinders or complements your character's attitude. Leave yourself open to inconsistencies. Your character's not God; he or she can become confused, can wonder, can hope for guidance, can feel conflicted. There's not a major character in all literature who doesn't spend most of his or her time striving for clarity or love or food or power or something. Why shouldn't the actor share some of those struggles?

Whatever happens to us while we're working on a role is *the one real truth we are all capable of admitting.* It may feel positive, it may feel negative; we're not to judge it, we're to express it. Regardless of what it leads to.

I was once rehearsing the play *Dial M for Murder* in a summer stock production, playing the lead role of the murderer, who is the epitome of cool, elegant aplomb. I was only twenty-four, and didn't feel elegant or cool. The actress cast as my wife was far more experienced and vivacious than me, and, I thought, far too old for me to be credibly married to. By the third day, my anxieties about being cast out of my depth were so high I was beginning to sweat and lose my voice during rehearsals. As we started a drinking scene early in the first act, the prop master handed out strange-looking glasses to each of us. I'd never handled anything like them before (they were brandy snifters, I later found out). All my cohorts seemed perfectly at ease with them, so I watched them surreptitiously and tried to do what they did until—the moment came for me to drink a toast.

As I tilted the glass onto my lip I suddenly realized, in horror, that my nose was inside the rim of the glass. I froze. I knew everyone was looking at me—especially my too-old actress-wife.

The director called to me, "Allan, what's the matter?"

My hand slowly removed the glass. I shuddered and began to shiver, sweat covering my face. My voice was pinched. "I'm sorry, Fred. I can't do this part. I'm sorry."

And I walked off, dizzy and shaken. One of the apprentices tried to help but I pushed him away. By then Fred, the director, was beside me. Very quietly, his hand on my shoulder to steady me, he asked "What happened? Everything was going fine."

I shook my head, tears welling up. "I'm not right for this, Fred. I'm too young, I don't have enough experience. I don't even know how to handle a damn drinking glass!"

"What're you talking about? There was nothing wrong with the way you held the glass. And you're not too young..."

I cut him off. "Didn't you see me? Didn't you see where my nose was? I couldn't even get it outside the glass to drink!"

Fred stared at me, dumbfounded. Then a realization flickered in his eyes. "I understand," he said. "You're right about the glass. Can I have it a moment?"

I handed it over. It was empty; we'd only been pantomiming

the drinking at that point. He called to the apprentice, "Would you please get me a drink of water?"

The apprentice stepped away to a sink in the rehearsal room. Fred kept talking: "It's okay, Allan. We can fix it, relax." Then he leaned close and whispered, "By the way, you may not know it, but your leading lady is crazy about you." I knew he was really trying to butter me up, but by then, the apprentice was back. Fred took the glass. "Allan, watch."

My eyes were glued to the glass as he raised it to his mouth. And suddenly there it was: him, too. His nose was inside the rim of that glass. I couldn't believe it. He handed it to the apprentice. "Take a sip," he said.

The fellow did. He couldn't get his nose out of the glass either.

"Now c'mere." Fred guided me to the sink. He picked up a used coffee container someone had left, rinsed it out, half-filled it with water, and gave it to me. "Take a sip from this."

I brought it right up to drink. And froze again. Just for an instant. Then put it down.

"Everybody's nose goes inside the rim. Right?" Fred asked.

I nodded. I felt like an idiot.

"Allan, you've gotten yourself into a state where your anxieties are ruling you. Stop dwelling on what you think you can't do. *If you're feeling lost, then so is the character.* What might he use to make himself feel better? Or what can you think of that might make you feel more elegant and above-it-all? You know how to work. Now get to it." Then he addressed the cast. "We're taking a ten-minute break, everybody."

I walked out behind the building, out on the grass underneath some trees, and thought about the issue: What might the character do if he felt at a loss? Drink. Go out and play tennis (he was a professional tennis player). That's an idea, I could come in carrying a tennis racket and work-out bag. But I don't really know how to play tennis, so those objects would just be props for me. Well then, what sort of sensory choice could get me to behave and feel as I want him to?

The object came zooming into my mind: yachting sneakers. As a kid, the furthest out I'd ever gotten into footwear was high-topped Keds. But as an adult, when I could afford to buy what I liked, I'd always hankered after a pair of those soft canvas sneakers that I saw elegant-looking men wear on boats. I never actually bought a pair, but I'd often imagined how cool and refined they might make me feel.

Back into the rehearsal hall I sauntered, light-footed and at ease. The more I imagined myself in those sneakers, the freer my behavior became. I even began to enjoy the prospect of a more experienced wife. But if I hadn't admitted my dilemma, damning as it was, I might never have been helped to a creative solution.

In rehearsals, how we feel always leads to how we behave. When we are on guard, so is our work; when we are open about ourselves, what we do becomes flowing and accessible.

Actors are not necessarily expected to be at ease during rehearsals, we are expected to be ready to work.

One of the primary difficulties in early working rehearsals is clarifying communication between actors and directors. When a director tells an actor "Your character is feeling very guilty here," are you supposed to try to look as if you're guilty? Do you try quickly to pick an incident from your life in which you were made to feel guilty? What do you do with such a direction?

Your first order of business is to *translate* what's been said.

When we were young children in school, a teacher might have said to any of us, "Sit still." We knew even then that the teacher didn't mean literally still—we'd have to be dead. She really meant still enough not to distract or disturb whatever else was going on.

If someone in a fit of anger yelled "Drop dead, you son-of-a-bitch," the translation of that might be something like, "Get out of my life, you mean, arrogant, lying cheat."

No word is necessarily literal. "Yes" can be "Yes, if you do what I want." "Go away" can generate a reply like "Gladly, but how far?" "I'm glad you're here" can mean "Now that I see you, I won't worry about your being sick."

To respond to the director's request for guilt, you have to question the kind and degree of whatever circumstances your character has been involved in, so you know what kind of guilt you're looking for. The guilt that Raskolnikov feels in *Crime and Punishment* for murdering an old woman is totally unlike the guilt Woody Allen typically assumes for just about everything in his films. The guilt the character undergoes may be like your experience when you hit and killed a small animal with your car during a night drive. Or it might be much like the continuing, nagging guilt we all sometimes carry when we don't remember our parents' anniversary or birthdays.

Once you've determined the area of guilt, you can try various means to act it, including physical forms that guilt can assume in your body: a migraine headache or a feeling of pressure throughout your body like a sinus blockage. You could also explore the possibilities of what a character like yours might do to look *un*guilty—what people in life tend to do when caught in a guilty act. Some try to laugh it off; some have trouble breathing, so they end up snorting in an effort to catch their breath; some will make every effort to distract their accuser.

A director or a producer in a rehearsal might say, "Look happier, would you?" Do you suddenly try to extend a smile, pulling all the necessary facial muscles into a frozen look of happiness? No. Search for a child's smile—perhaps your own child's, or you when you were much younger—and invest yourself with that youngster's pleasures. Think of someone or some event that could awaken a fuller measure of pleasure for the character or yourself. And if you find real resistance to this "happy look," first let yourself think lousy, unhappy thoughts or images. Let them infuse you, then act the reverse: let all those misery-inducing images disappear. It will only take a few seconds to accomplish.

When directors talk to you, either about the play or your role in it, be open to anything they say that touches upon your thematic idea or its opposite. Be prepared to acknowledge any suggestion, even if it doesn't tally with your initial concept. Give the director enough credibility to follow out his or her ideas. Try to fulfill them. Your theme isn't written in granite; it can adjust to change. That's what good rehearsals are for. All the artists involved should have ideas that can be plumbed. It can be exciting to be engaged by someone else's idea.

As a director, I've often had to work with actors who needed coaching to reach fruition in a role. Either because of poor training, insular training (by which the actor claims the privilege of having only one way to work, and it's not the way I, the director, am currently privy to), or from lack of experience on stage, these actors stay tight and resistant with their bodies and feelings throughout rehearsals. And because the pressure of time hasn't allowed me to lead them into warm-ups and/or improvisations that might loosen their imaginations and behavior, I dictate ways of behaving for their characters, outlining the roles directorially, hoping they will eventually fill in the outline. Sometimes, depending on how evocative my stipulations have been, the actors flourished. Other times, my dictates led to resentment, and the actors became even tighter.

We all, actors and directors, have to try to stay open-minded and adaptable to each other's agendas. As of this writing, I've never been fired as an actor. (I have had a few occasions, however, when the director stopped speaking to me.) I discovered early on that if I first tried to carry out the director's wishes and visions, I was then freer to explore possibilities that came from me. Many times my ideas were turned down, many more times they led to a collaboration with the director. That sense of communion, of mutual interest in different concepts and their execution, is central to any theatrically creative endeavor.

Elia Kazan proved this one day while moderating a session of the Playwrights Unit at the Actors Studio. (There were several units at the Studio, only one of which was for actors exclusively.)

On this particular day, a young director was presenting a new one-act play with two actors. When the piece was over, Kazan addressed the director, trying to clarify the work. In no time, the director was blaming the actors for not fulfilling his instructions. The actors made it clear that the director constantly interfered with their efforts. As the argument grew, a young man in the audience suddenly stood up and called out, "Mr. Kazan, Mr. Kazan, this is all pointless. I'm the author and I don't know what any of these people were doing with my play. Nothing up there was what I wrote!"

We were all entertained by this burgeoning mess. But Kazan was extremely considerate. Without any hint of blame, he elicited from the director that there had been no communication with the playwright during rehearsal. The director simply assumed he understood the play. Kazan quietly prodded the actors: "You really think you could have done the play better without the director, don't you?" The actors nodded yes. Kazan turned to the director again: "And you really feel that with a better choice of actors you could fulfill the material?" The director nodded.

The playwright was getting ready to explode, but Kazan caught him with "And you, sir, you believe you understand what you wrote far better than the actors or the director?"

The playwright was vigorous in his reply. "I certainly do."

Kazan smiled and nodded. "Okay. I think this gives us all a chance to find out something very important."

He turned to the actors. "Why don't you two work on this piece all by yourselves? No director, just you. Then bring it in."

Without stopping for any response or effect, he swung to the director. "You really didn't have the support you needed from these two, so how about if I get you a couple of actors who will do exactly what you want—and don't worry about anything the writer said here today, you just bring in your vision of the piece. Will you do that?" The director agreed.

Kazan then turned to the playwright. "And I'm going to do the same for you, sir. I will find two actors perfectly willing to act anything you believe necessary to fulfill your play. You just tell them what to do. Is that all right with you?"

"Great," answered the playwright. "That's fabulous."

"And we'll schedule all three versions for the same day," said Kazan. "That should be quite a day."

It certainly was. Word of the event had gone out, and three weeks later, when the scheduled day rolled around, there was a standing-room-only crowd.

The actors went first. Then the director. Then the playwright. All three versions were terrible. The actors' work was full of moments—small, valuable emotional or behavioral sequences that were individually interesting—but added up to nothing more. There was no sense of what the play was about.

It was clear from the director's work that he indeed had his own vision of the play, a vision which he had forced his actors to carry out. But there were no redeeming human characteristics or qualities in the performances. The actors were merely there to execute the director's idea of the play, and had left out all individual niceties of feeling and thought.

The playwright's version was truly the most lifeless. The actors hardly moved, or even behaved. And when they spoke, they sounded as if they were trying to imitate line readings demonstrated by the writer. It was horrible.

When Kazan asked for comments, a few people tried to be kind to each of the participants, but almost no one spoke of the end results.

Except Kazan, who came right out with it: "None of them really worked, did they?" He was very warm about it. "You all tried your best, we saw that. But I guess this sums up what all of us have already learned but keep forgetting: that at its best, and at its worst, theater is a giant compromise. Nobody ever gets only what he wants."

Keep this truth in the backs of your mind whenever you're on a job. It will help in some of those dark days when you find yourself at odds with your director or author. It should never deter you from doing your best to carry out whatever you are working on as richly as you can. It's only to remind you that we are all fallible, and we must all reserve the right to fail. You can never find out what is right until you've tried out what may be wrong. The measure of all actors is not how much anyone agrees or disagrees with their interpretation, but how well they carry it out.

Another dilemma we all face at early rehearsals is how to deal with our fellow actors. We're all relative strangers at this point. We may be somewhat familiar with one another, but not enough to feel as free as we would be with friends of long standing. We tend to be rather anxious and concerned about everyone's reactions to us as both individuals and actors. Unfortunately, most directors do very little to create a climate in which we might feel creatively disposed to one another (directors are usually busy with their own anxieties). For a director, the first reading of the script is usually meant as an excuse to get started, or as a sounding board for the director and/or producer to hear the piece read as a whole, and as a test of their casting.

As actors, not only do most of us come together as relative

strangers, we also tend to read the material totally out of context. The characters in the piece have lives and relationships to one another that exist prior to when their lives in the play or film begin. The author has been privy to these private lives, but the actors haven't been. So what we usually get at first rehearsals or readings is strangers trying to relate to one another without any benefit of prior lives or circumstances—real or fictional—to speak of or from.

Which explains why not very much occurs at the first few rehearsals.

To break this initial coolness and lack of connection when starting rehearsals, some actors will suggest going out together for a cup of coffee or a drink. Or the producer will have a tableful of fruit, crackers, bagels, peanut butter, coffee, and tea available for cast members, not only on the first day of rehearsal, but continually thereafter.

This kind of effort to help break the ice is very human, but not creatively channeled toward the work. As a matter of fact, the presumption that actors must feel comfortable (i.e. well-fed and taken care of) to enter into relationships demanded by the script is not even necessarily true.

Friendships and ease of behavior in life are measured by the degree of intimacies shared. It usually takes a long period of time or a mutually crucial experience for human beings to establish trusting relationships. Actors don't have the luxury of such time before or during rehearsals, and I am certainly not going to suggest that you get involved with your fellow actors in an automobile accident just to be able to share some circumstances.

What is needed for actors to trust one another in rehearsal is something quite different: *an equal display of daring.* You can't have one actor trying out behavior for his role while another actor denigrates those efforts. If one actor inclines toward an unexpected interpretation, and the other actor becomes cool or defensive toward him, only tension and distance will result between them.

When this issue became focused for me, I began to question myself: under what circumstances in life do any of us find ourselves able to say and/or do things which, under ordinary circumstances, we would not allow ourselves to say or do in front of complete strangers? Immediately I thought of being drunk, or being under the influence of drugs. Or just having undergone a traumatic experience, such as the death of a loved one, or being robbed and beaten, or raped, or...my mind raced on to one awful experience after another, none of which seemed conducive to an open and flowing relationship.

Then I remembered my trip to Europe years earlier on an ocean liner. Many times I would find myself on the deck, or at meals, or at a card table, trading innumerable details of my life with all sorts of people, sometimes even exaggerating or actually lying about what I had done and experienced. I became, almost instantly, a sharing, daring human being, readily open to almost everyone about me, and willing to accept anything they said in return. I never questioned anyone's stories or behavior. There was an allowance and a generosity of spirit that flowed from me toward everyone, and I felt the reverse to be equally true.

Every one of my shared and open relationships on this voyage began the same way: "Where are you from?" or a variation thereof. Either I asked it, or the other person did. It never seemed to matter if we were from different regions or the same ones. It started with a general area, and in minutes we were discussing where we were born, what our parents were like, whether we were married, children or no children, occupations, and then on into incredibly intimate details of our lives, such as why we divorced, how we felt about vivisection, what we wanted to accomplish with our lives. The more we met on the ship, the more wide-ranging our discussions. And by the time we docked, whole lives had interacted. (Once on shore, almost every one of those ship-time relationships faded or dimmed considerably.)

This strange (yet familiar) maritime openness has also happened to me on trains, buses, and planes. Whenever people leave old ground, a very human need to voice familiarities seems to arise; quite differently than at a party or a pre-planned dinner. At most social functions, we all expect to trade information about vocations, interests, or public family details. The food, the drinks, and the music are elements designed to encourage chatter or wit or networking. This other venturing—by boat, plane, or train— always has in it the possibility of no future contact. The only time

I would ever commune with these human beings was for this short period, so I was more prone to expose my more hidden, personal self to them.

I began to use this idea as a kick-off for scene work with actors who seemed unable to bring much of themselves to rehearsals. I suggested that two actors bring in a scene they had each read separately, but not yet together, so that each was familiar with whatever took place in the scene. They were also to make no effort to memorize their lines, so that it would be truly a reading when they brought it in.

Instead of then going directly to an acting choice, such as picking a quality for the character or an emotional subject to get the actors vulnerable, I asked each of them to pick a place they had known many years earlier. To help choose such a place, I suggested one related to the idea of family. (I might just as readily have suggested any number of other subjects: friendship, school, business, betrayal, luxury, etc.)

The actors were asked to verbally share only physical details of their respective places with each other. If it was a house, where was it located, how many rooms, what colors was it painted, how tall, any trees around it, what kinds of smells inhabited it, what happened to it in different weathers—during rain, snowstorms, hot spells. What was it like living and working or playing in this house? What kinds of people lived in it or visited it? What kinds of clothes did people wear in it? What kinds of food were eaten? Were there any special occasions when food and dress changed?

The actors were not to tell who the people were or any feelings involved, only to describe and share physical details. Each actor was to compare the details of his or her place to those of the partner's place. If one actor said her house was two stories high, the other actor would say his house was only one story or his was also two stories—or he might reply that there was no house at all in his place. If one said there were four trees, the other might say there were no trees, but several flowering bushes. So that regularly they were trading details and comparing their places.

The only other stipulation was that the actors were to speak very conversationally and make no effort to project out to those of us who were watching.

After several minutes, when I felt they were in a real discussion of their places and their bodies were relaxed and expressive, I asked them to maintain focus on their respective places, to silently think over everything they had already heard and told one another, and to consider other details they had not yet spoken of. And while they were doing that, I asked them to begin reading the dialogue, leaving themselves open to any possible connections between the places they'd been sharing with each other, and the words they were about to speak.

Instantly there was life between the actors. There were thoughts; there were reactions and observations. They smiled, they laughed, they considered, they were solemn. Responses were spontaneous and everchanging. They sounded real and unafraid, un-self-conscious. Trusting. Quiet, but true. And a genuine relationship developed. The trading of facts about their places had acted as a conduit that enabled them, strangers at the beginning, to interact familiarly. The places also provided a mutual context from which the actors could explore. No matter if they became lost or unsure in the dialogue, they always had their respective places accessible. The places provided a repository for real thoughts—not manufactured thoughts about their hardly-begun parts and their fictional dialogue, but concrete, specific thoughts (and thereby impulses), stimulated by reference to actual places and circumstances.

This technique makes even the first rehearsals a real adventure: ideas and images for dealing with the characters, the text, and the situations begin to flow. And a difficult, anxiety-producing dilemma can be averted in a very short, productive time.

Another technique for stirring empathies between you and your fellow actors in those early rehearsals: secrets. Is there a person who doesn't have some? Characters must have secrets, too, beyond what the authors have given us. If we provide ourselves as actors with mutual secrets, chosen beforehand, what might that lead to as we rehearse?

Suppose I said to two actors about to start rehearsing a scene, "You both now know that one of you—as a person, not a character—has been and still is slightly retarded. Pick either yourself or your partner. Make a choice and stick to it."

If you pick yourself, consider any incidents in which you functioned poorly at any time in your life, fumbles you made in speaking, forgetting people's names, awkwardness in physical movements—

you'll find ammunition to make this premise plausible. (Just think: it could be true about any of us if our parents and teachers never told us.)

If you choose your partner, mull over any behavior or attitudes you've observed about him or her that would be symptomatic of retardation. Then start your rehearsal and see if you or your partner does or says anything to support the choice you made.

It's wonderfully helpful not to tell each other whom you chose. You may actually have chosen each other—that doesn't matter. What matters is that you've created a real secret between you. You both know only what it's about, not who your partner has chosen, or what it's going to lead to.

Your next time through the script, you can even change your choice, or you can pretend to, but really use your first one. You'll still have a real secret.

I've used this technique as an actor and director in classes, rehearsals, on camera, and on stage—always with stimulating results. Soon after instigating the process in a professional class I taught, one of the actors in the class (a woman) and I were both hired for the same soap opera, "One Life to Live," and found ourselves having a scene together. We decided to try this secret idea for our first rehearsal, and chose possible retardation for one of us. Without telling anyone.

The scene had me (as a lawyer) being summoned to her apartment to discuss her sister's will, which I had drawn up. It was a cat-and-mouse scene anyway, but when we added our own cat-and-mouse secret, we laughed in places we never expected to, we caught every look in each other's eyes, every inflection of tone and voice. When we finished, the director was impressed. He said, "I don't know what you two were up to, but just keep doing it."

Secrets to use can be physical: you both now know that one part of your body is made of plastic (which could have been implanted when either of you was an infant). The secrets can relate to your future: you both now know that as of midnight tonight one of you is going to give up acting forever. They can be metaphysical: you both now know that in a week one of you is going to be capable of raising up the dead.

By using secrets, you provide your character with inner concerns and impulses that can add insights and vivacity to scenes. If you don't like the result of one secret, try another. And if your scene partner doesn't wish to join in, try a secret on your own. Write it out on a piece of masking tape and hide it inside your partner's dressing room. Or whisper it through his or her keyhole; then as far as you know, that person has heard it.

Another way to push aside inhibitions and the caution that many actors bring to rehearsals is to rehearse your role as if the character were written in a very Italian way—big gestures and rolling shoulders. Include the accent, it'll help move you past sounding literary.

Try some German. Get your voice more guttural and commanding, Nazi-like. Get yourself some French intonations and gestures, or Spanish ones. You'd be surprised how behaving more gaucho-like, twirling-skirted, bedroom-eyed, or bedroom-voiced will help release impulses usable for your role.

When all your acting choices have been tried, when the director finally leaves you mainly to your own devices, when the working rehearsals give way to the necessities of run-throughs and you're approaching dress rehearsals, you might want to try a sit-down speed-through.

That means you go through everything you've structured so far for your role—all the values you can maintain, the emotions, the atti-tudes—while you say your lines to one another as fast as you can. If you stumble with the words, or forget some of your lines, use gibberish or noises to keep up the verbal pace until you remember what's miss-ing or your partner moves you ahead to a line you do remember.

A speed-through will suddenly loosen impulses, thoughts, and feel-ings for your part that you didn't even know you had. But even more importantly, the speed-through gives you a sense of your character's relationship to the whole play. It either validates your theme or helps you redefine it. And it's a wonderful preparation for the tightrope we all have to walk in front of an audience or the camera—when, despite our best intentions, some of our work is always discarded. If we rehearsed well, though, what's left will be pretty damned impressive.

There is an immutable triangle at work in the affairs of most of us. To decide which clothes to wear on a given day you don't just grab something. Not really. First you check the weather, then you consider the condition of any garments lying around from the pre-vious day. You think over what you're going to be doing, who you might be seeing, how long you'll be out, what colors you wore yesterday, and God knows what else, depending on your haberdashery habits. What you actually do is cast your thoughts backward before you move forward with your selections.

Think of yourself basking on one of the smaller, uncrowded Hawaiian beaches. You know you're having a lovely time, but to really relish your treat in the island sun, all you need do is remind yourself of what life was like back on your old Chicago streets in winter. We do that, consciously or unconsciously, all the time. It's a fact of life. Now how do you transfer this process to acting?

Think of the script as your future: that's what you want to get to. The present is you, right there wherever you are, open to whatever is around you. The past can't be just any old portion of your life, it has to have some relevance to where you want to get to—right? Wrong. Once you've read that material, it starts cooking all by itself somewhere in your subconscious. *So any choice of subject from your past*—place, person, incident, sensory condition, book, painting, or piece of music—will have relevance. You've just got to trust that you wouldn't even have thought of using it if it weren't pertinent somehow. Once you're working on a script, everything you do that happens to you will either be to move you toward the material or away from it. But it will be relevant.

It's like sailing. To navigate a sailboat from one point to another against the wind, you use a series of maneuvers called tacking. Tacking means that instead of heading the boat straight toward its objective, you steer it at an angle away from that objective to use the wind most efficiently. In other words, you use the wind to keep the boat moving forward by zig-zagging its way toward its goal. At any one of these zig-zag movements, a person ignorant of sailing technique might legitimately ask, "What are you doing? You're going away from your objective, not toward it." Which is exactly what anyone could say about an artist's search for the truths of his conception: "Why are you doing this when I thought you were supposed to be accomplishing that?"

Think of all the sketches Michelangelo must have gone through before he decided on God's finger transferring life to man in his painting on the ceiling of the Sistine Chapel; many of them probably had nothing to do with that finger.

I have a book showing Picasso at work. One section is a series of sketches leading to a final painting of a scene at a beach. The very first sketch shows the ordinary juxtapositions of sun, sky, water, sand, people, and boats. By the final painting the sun has *become* the beach and the people are nearly obliterated.

The actor has to learn that the craft, as well as the art, of acting is more like the process of sailing than a straight-on intellectual or logical pursuit of something in the script.

We have to learn to trust the right side of our brains, the hemisphere in which all our unlogical, often unconscious, but always personal connections with life reside. The left part of our brain, the rational part that knows how to speak and do math, is pretty thoroughly trained by the time we reach adulthood. It's that right side that needs more nourishment and use, to keep us from always doing the sensible and expected things in life.

And just as it is the unexpected incidents along the way that make a good trip memorable, so it is the unexpected discoveries while working on your role that make your creative life more stimulating and worthwhile.

Sarah Siddons, an accomplished actress of the nineteenth century and by all contemporary accounts the greatest Lady Macbeth ever seen, relates that during her rehearsal period, the sleepwalking scene in the play continually eluded her. One night, when her family was already asleep and while laboring fruitlessly in the attic where she worked, she decided to rest her mind. She took her candle and began descending the steps to her room. A sudden gust of wind blew out the candle, and she found herself alone in the dark. Disturbed and fearful, she continued her descent, gripping the railing so as not to fall, and treading lightly enough not to awaken any of her loved ones. Hardly breathing and feeling close to peril, she made her way down, and realized, there in the dark, what a wonderfully fitting image her thoughts and behavior on the steps would be for Lady Macbeth's nocturnal wandering. That's what she used for her performance.

Like Mrs. Siddons, many actors have had this inspirational impetus to their work occur when they had given up the direct pursuit of their objectives. Instead, they were absorbed in something entirely different, or were resting their minds. Inspiration hardly ever flows in a straight line.

You must leave room for your wanderings. While you're working on any of your acting tasks, you cannot judge yourself, or be
judged, as if that exploration were your performance. You should
be trying out the tasks you are using, and "which ways the winds
are blowing" that day. If the results are not to anyone's liking,
including your own, you'll simply change the task. But you must
allow yourself complete leeway to try out anything that will lead
you to your final destination.

In rehearsals, you have to juggle at least two different tasks
before you add a third or a fourth. In previous chapters, I've
described three different areas of acting work—situation, character, and text—that need to be fused to arrive at a performance.
But there is no magic formula that guarantees results if you begin
with a situation task, then a character idea, then add the lines.
That's too linear. Each piece you rehearse will, and should, set off
different stimuli. Each rehearsal environment may encourage different choices. And each rehearsal will present different opportunities to try out various areas of work.

If you got the role of Quasimodo in the play or film version of
The Hunchback of Notre Dame, you should begin by asking yourself questions about the part, including: how does Quasimodo
live in the church? What are his chores? When and what does he
eat, and with whom? Does he eat alone? Does he have a room of
his own? How deformed is he besides the hump on his back? Can
he wash himself? How do others treat him? Whom does he
admire? Whom does he obey? These are all questions having to
do with Quasimodo's life before the action of the piece even
begins. And many of these questions will lead to improvisations
on your own, to help define the answers. (Improvisations that can
be done privately and in public, well before official rehearsals are
called.)

And the same is true for trying out characteristics and attitudes
for the character. Does Quasimodo speak more like a retarded
person, or a very bright-minded being with a severe vocal impedi-
ment? Which choice gives you more options as you explore his
relationships during the course of the play? Does he regard his
humped back as a punishment from God, or as a terrible accident
of life? (Which gives him more vitality and complexity when he

finally saves Esmeralda's life and kills his keeper?) What pains him? What pleases him? What are his dreams? What are his secrets? What images come to mind as you ask these questions?

Make lists of all the physical facts that are stated about the character: the attitudes expressed by him, all the qualities that are spoken of him by others. Begin practicing all of these elements outside of regular rehearsals as soon and as continuously as you can. In no particular order. Just so you cover everything on your lists.

Take these images and ideas with you wherever you go and *practice* using them in your own life. See which ones last, which ones become the most suggestive for you, which ones you enjoy trying out over and over. Those you find wanting or too alien, leave out, and look for alternate choices. Or reverse choices. If it seems certain that Quasimodo is devoid of sexual desires, start your work on him by being extremely sensual, then after a while, choose not to show it. Or once you've established his sexuality, behave in an opposite way.

Whichever factors and qualities and attitudes encourage you to be ongoing and flowing in your work are the ones to proceed with. Those that don't stir you should be left behind. You'll find others.

With this body of explorations already in progress when you are called to rehearse, make sure *you* are available. Check yourself, relax, make a choice of place or person, or a smell, or a song that's personal to you, add in a choice for the character, and as the rehearsal proceeds, begin to juggle, and keep juggling as you read through the script. Let your choices influence you; let the feelings, thoughts, and impulses that arise weave in and around the words of the text and the ways you relate to the actors rehearsing with you. Any images that continue to come to mind— *add them in.*

If you're not actually involved in scenes that are being rehearsed, choose one of the character's basic qualities, such as his gullibility, and keep that quality alive and available in you as you observe and relate to other people at the rehearsal. Or go off on the side and try improvising on one of the physical chores that the character might do daily, like cleaning his keeper's room.

Pantomime it. Try to imagine and feel what his hands might be like after years of scrubbing floors, what kinds of strengths or weaknesses might be in his knees, what smells he always has about him.

I once did a scene from Eugene O'Neill's *Beyond the Horizon*, a play about two brothers, one who wants to travel the world, the other drawn to life on a farm. By an accident of fate, each is given the wrong wish.

I played the adventure-desiring guy, now stuck miserably as a farmer with a family. Since I had no experience whatsoever of farming, I used the wooden parquet floor of my New York apartment as imaginary planting rows. I established the sensory conditions of hot sun and unshaded distances around me, chose an old tattered work shirt and pants and worn boots as my costume, picked a 6:30 A.M. time, and began pantomiming digging and laying out seeds on a summer day. I never settled on one kind of seed, I planted whichever sort popped into my mind—potato, tomato, it didn't matter.

As I plied my way down each row of parquet, I began to telescope the time: my first few minutes became his first hour, my second few minutes another hour, and so on. In my sensory imagination, the sun rose and became hotter and hotter as my imaginary hours progressed. I encouraged my body to accumulate the sensory results of this advancing heat, the sweating across my forehead, scalp, and back of my neck, the clinging of my shirt, the heat gathering in my crotch and boots, the thick dryness in my mouth, the focus of my eyes becoming narrow and painful, the lack of breeze, the lack of water, the lack of sounds, the sudden flight of birds, to remind me of how grounded I was.

Within half an hour, I felt I'd worked this way for weeks; after a couple of days of rehearsing, I believed I'd been at it for years. By the time we did the scene and I entered my character's farmhouse at the end of his workday, my body dictated his needs for water and solace far beyond anything I might have considered without that practice. And my character's need for going *Beyond the Horizon* was intensified tenfold.

Keep facets of the character available for you to try out as you are called in to rehearsals. Always start with one of your personal choices, then add one of the character's. After a while, make two different choices. Repeat the two new ones, then go back to the first two. See which ones stay provocative, which ones add to your feelings and impulses, which ones give you insights into the role.

When you are able to keep two choices going at a time, add a third: two for your character, one for you. Remember, your choices should be like the poles used by skiers in a slalom. Skiers don't try to hit those poles, they curve around them and in between them. The poles structure their progress down the course. Your acting choices are to lead you on, to create real thoughts and feelings for you to use; they are stepping stones to the material, the means that enable you to explore. They are the process, not the goal.

The more proficient you become with adding more and more choices for your roles, the freer you'll be to experience the duality that takes place for a master craftsman in any medium—when the work you are doing actually transports your self into another plane of experience, a high that no drug or drink can come close to.

There is a superb rendering of this experience in the movie *Visions of Eight.* Eight noted film directors were asked to choose their own subjects at the 1972 Olympics and shoot a short film on that subject.

Each film was fascinating, but the particular segment that struck me most was directed by Arthur Penn. The subject he chose was the men's pole vault, a sport about which I had little prior knowledge. In Penn's film, there were several slow-motion sequences depicting the enormous skills required of a champion pole vaulter, skills that were a real revelation to me. As the athletes raced down the course, their flesh was pressed against the bone masks of their faces from air pressure, exactly like the faces of astronauts being malformed as they reached speeds of Mach I and Mach II. The athletes' concentration stayed absolute. Their arms balanced their poles precariously, their legs drummed into the earth, their hearts thudded in their chests, their breaths pumped ferociously for more oxygen. Then, at the end of their runs, came the incredible sequences of them uplifting themselves on their poles—poles that hardly looked sturdy enough, poles that bent and swayed and propelled their bodies like projectiles high into the air. There were close-ups of the athletes' faces straining ever harder, ever more fiercely than during their runs, as they twisted and willed their bodies ever higher to clear the bar at the top of the measuring stand.

Athlete after athlete failed, an arm or a foot or a leg dislodging that thin-barred validation of their efforts. And at each of these failed attempts, the athlete looked agonized and torn. But then one man cleared the bar. The look of exaltation on his face and in his body was unforgettable; he seemed beatified, floating to the earth on a cushion of air, utterly at peace, alone and Godlike, at one with everything worthwhile in the universe.

I suddenly understood why athletes everywhere find it worth the struggle to achieve such a wondrous state, the exaltation that human beings are capable of when they have mastered a skill and can give themselves over to the experience of their accomplishment.

The concert film *Monterey Pop* featured, among many American rock and folk performers, a musician from India, sitar player Ravi Shankar. Amidst all the free-wheeling, spontaneous, musically dynamic, and personally exciting artists captured in the film, there was a single sequence during the Shankar piece that truly astounded me (and the rest of the movie audience the night I saw it).

It was at least halfway into the film that Shankar and his fellow musicians appeared. One terrific performer after another had aroused the actual concert audience, as well as the movie theater audience, to wild applause, dancing, vocal shrieks, and howls of delight. Several performers were clearly playing at the top of their form, and some of their singing and stage behavior seemed limited only by the physical limitations of their vocal cords and muscles.

When Shankar was introduced, there was a better-than-respectful response from both audiences. As he began to play his sitar (which resembled an oversized guitar), his concentration and skill absorbed all of us. The piece began slowly, almost evenly. The musicians playing the tabla (a small, drumlike instrument played with the hands) and tamboura (a drone instrument that kept the rhythms) both took their impetus from Shankar.

The composition began to build. Shankar's fingers began to fly from string to string. A terrific run of notes on those twelve strings started. And continued. And continued. And continued. Both Shankar and the musician playing the tabla had their eyes closed. The woman tamboura player's eyes were open, but inwardly focused, feeling the music, finding her place in it. Their concentrations were ferocious: nostrils were flaring, lips and jaw muscles strained, eyebrows shifted and were shaken by an incredible variety of feelings. Their heads bobbed and weaved, their necks shrank and extended, pushed and pulled by the torrent of sensations within. The tension in all of us watching was almost unbearable. It seemed impossible to sustain such a run.

All of a sudden, still playing, still building, as if by a secret connecting thread, Shankar and the tabla player opened their eyes, looked at one another, and smiled—radiant, life-giving smiles. The entire audience erupted with loving howls of pleasure. Shankar immediately turned to the lady on the tamboura, and miraculously, she was there, looking right at him, her beautiful smile joining his, her face flushing almost to the color of the red caste mark on her forehead.

Their smiles passed from one to the other, transported by the music they were playing. And we, the happiest of audiences, applauded and laughed and looked at each other, some unbelieving, some equally transformed, some standing and swaying, trying to find our place in the glorious music that rushed at us and into us.

The end of the piece brought bedlam of the most loving kind. The shouts and the applause wouldn't end. To be witness to such skill and such humanity at the same time was to be in the presence of greatness. Their smiles—like Charlie Chaplin's at the end of *City Lights*, when the blind girl, now able to see, realizes that Chaplin's Little Tramp was the one responsible for her regaining her vision—are the real lights of all our lives.

Only great craft, the mastering of their instruments and their techniques, allowed these artists to exist so fully within their playing.

It is within all our grasps to practice diligently enough to achieve such a liberation of spirit within our own works. First comes our self, then come choices. Then comes practice. But I want to say this again: the hinge that keeps the door open to inspiration while you are acting is to allow your own thoughts, feelings, and sensations to become expressible. Never presume that you have less to offer a role than others. You have differences, and you must keep your differences alive and available.

If there is one great rule that governs all good actors it is that once a choice has been made—be it for the sleepwalking scene of Lady Macbeth by Mrs. Siddons, for details of behavior (such as those Robert De Niro used for Travis Bickle in *Taxi Driver*, that Marlon Brando used for Stanley in *A Streetcar Named Desire*, or that Ingrid Bergman used for Ilsa in *Casablanca*), or for any memorable performance on stage or film—you carry it out as beautifully and as richly as you can. Invest yourself in your choices: they come from you, they must include you. Trust in your own originality.

Great writers command our respect because they are able to reveal the layers of thought and impulse that contribute to the feelings of the characters they write about. Great painters help us to comprehend and feel life through the perceptiveness of their visions and brushwork. Great actors are capable of illuminating the psychological and emotional lives of the characters they play in ways that can surpass the most erudite and incisive therapists or social workers. A critic once said that to see Edmund Kean, the great nineteenth-century actor, perform Hamlet, was like reading Shakespeare illuminated by lightning. Not a bad epitaph for any actor.

'Freedom

There I was, shortly after the end of World War II, only seventeen years old, driving a half-ton truck for the United States Army's 14th Quartermaster Corps in a Japanese farmland community northeast of Tokyo in the middle of a very bitter winter.

A battalion of us had disembarked six weeks earlier in Tokyo Bay as part of the early occupational forces in Japan. There was no fighting—the peace treaty had been signed—but everything Japanese was off-limits. Water had to be boiled before drinking; we ate mostly canned goods and powdered eggs and milk. Warnings were issued regularly to keep away from any of the local farmers' produce—and their rice whiskey. And no fraternizing.

Military police and guard patrols were omnipresent. We drove our trucks five days a week to all kinds of army outposts, some-times even making deliveries into the city of Tokyo itself. The MPs would flag us in, we'd make our drop, and they'd wave us on our way. Tokyo was a hidden domain.

Wherever we drove, Japanese of every age bowed down to our vehicles as we passed by. When we stopped at a crossing, we could hear their litanies of obeisance as they humbled themselves. It was a disturbing image for a Brooklyn-born kid who had never traveled further than New Jersey, but who had been conditioned to hate and fear the Japanese during four years of war.

I had never driven a truck, or even a car, before this army assignment. There was never a vehicle as eccentric and cumber-some as our half-tons: no shock absorbers, gear boxes designed by a madman, and no doors or windows on the cabs, which made driving in twenty-degree weather with the wind whipping at us like living in the freezer compartment of a refrigerator with a fan on. Among the innumerable regulations governing our supply trips was the one stipulating that regardless of weather conditions, all vehicles were to be thoroughly hosed down upon final return to our depot. That invariably meant icicles and frost forming on every exposed part of our anatomies.

185

After our arctic hosings, we were allowed to return to our barracks: wooden, uninsulated, warped, draft-ridden tinder-box structures that formerly housed poor Japanese foot soldiers. The barracks were "heated" by wood-burning stoves, but to conserve wood in this war-impoverished area, no stoves were lit during the day except on weekends. Gathering firewood was a daunting prospect, given the tree-barren landscape. Every twig and stick within walking distance had disappeared long ago. What was left were army packing crates. Within days of my arrival, there was hardly a shipment delivered by our trucks still encased in its original wooden crate. We soon learned that no wood could be stored for the next day—it would be stolen by one of the non-truck drivers in the barracks nearby.

I had as much patriotic fervor as the next guy, but two months of this neverending cold-and-wet, bouncing-and-uncrating truck-driving life out in the boondocks was making all of us perverse and truculent. Arguments flared everywhere, trucks were getting into accidents (sometimes with each other), poor neighboring Japanese farmers were being robbed and beaten. Prostitutes at least kept the rape rate down. I wanted out of there badly.

One day, almost miraculously, in our barracks edition of the *Stars and Stripes*, the overseas newspaper, I saw a listing which read: "Actors wanted for Special Services, no prior experience necessary." I didn't know exactly what that meant, and I hardly read that part. It was the next phrase that caught me: "In Tokyo."

In Tokyo? Actors? Special Services? What was that? Who cared? It was in Tokyo. So what if everything Japanese was still supposed to be off-limits? There were enlisted men's clubs in Tokyo, there were shops, there were restaurants, there were even hotels. There were things to look at even if you couldn't touch.

What did I have to do? It said in the notice whom I had to see, but what would I have to *act?* I'd been in one college play—just before I enlisted—but that was just to date this girl I liked. Hey, maybe I could bluff my way through. (I was used to bluffing from growing up in the wilds of Brooklyn anyway.)

I wrangled a pass, caught a ride on one of our trucks going into the city, and went to the specified address, which turned out to be an office on the third floor of a great-looking Japanese theater, already renamed the Ernie Pyle Theater. Plays and musicals for all the enlisted men and officers in and around Tokyo were being produced. The office was not very crowded, but did have two beautiful young Japanese women as secretaries, who more than occupied my attention while I waited.

A captain appeared, jovial and quite friendly, interviewed me for several minutes, then asked me to read a monologue from some play I'd never heard of. I read intelligently, not emotionally or passionately, but clearly. The captain told me that I was very good, and that he'd like to have me join the company. (I later found out that there had been a total of six men who auditioned, and all of us were accepted.)

I was thrilled. I left the building and walked for hours, up and down every street nearby, out and around as far as I could go without losing sight of the Ernie Pyle. I walked for hours, soaking up the sounds, smells, and sights of this secret world of Japanese city culture.

It took almost two weeks for me to be assigned to the Special Service unit, so the first play I was scheduled to act in was already in rehearsal when I arrived. There was only a small role left for me (or maybe that's the one role they thought I could handle adequately), a doctor in the farce *Boy Meets Girl*. That was fine with me, because I didn't have the faintest idea of what I would do with a larger part anyway.

The camaraderie was great. Rehearsals were fun and interesting. Watching the Japanese scenic designer and his painters work was fascinating. The theater was wonderfully equipped. I was eating, drinking, and sleeping in an exotic environment. I was happy.

Then came the performances. Over a thousand GIs a night, some from the very same outfits I'd helped supply in my quartermaster days. Even guys from my old outfit came to see what I could do on a stage.

What they saw was blind, obliterating fright. Trembles, shivers, the sweats—my costume was drenched every performance. My throat was on fire from tension. I thanked God that I had only a few lines at a time. I was supposed to push a character onstage in a wheelchair; the first night, I almost pushed him into the orchestra pit. I felt as though I hadn't been potty-trained. I considered getting very ill to avoid going out there again. The director, a specially-assigned lieutenant, noticed my plight and suggested a shot of whiskey before going on. I told him I didn't drink. He said that made it even better—it would have more effect. I thought he meant good effect, so I swallowed it down. To this day, I don't remember that performance, but the other actors swore I did it. Oh, did they swear.

In the end, it was just single-minded, alley-cat survival instincts that kept me performing. I knew that if I didn't bull my way through, it was back to the truck and the icicles. As my somewhat naively aggressive persona kept butting up against the cultural and ethical consequences of playing the teenage conqueror, the one outlet I had for my mixed-up feelings was being in Special Services. Whereas some of my truckdriving comrades had taken to venting themselves and their frustrations on the people around them back in the boondocks, within a few weeks of performing in *Boy Meets Girl,* and then in a musical extravaganza we put into rehearsal, I found myself able to project many of my complicated feelings into the parts I was acting. My characters were allowed far more range of expression than I permitted myself. Just before or after a performance, my fears or doubts or foolishnesses or outbursts were not only condoned by those I worked with, they were encouraged. Never before in my life was I surrounded by so much support for anything I felt within me to be expressed. There were no rules for what our troupe of actors was allowed to say or feel.

Especially after a train tour of bases in Japan took us through Hiroshima. Nothing could have prepared us for that sight. Silence and awe were our responses. For days. And then did we cut loose, hooting and howling, cursing, and ranting epithets about God and man, heaven and hell. We made up songs about love and death and longing and children and mothers and fathers and war and weapons.

Our one base of sensibility was performing. It became an uplifting act of sharing to make our mostly teenage GI audiences laugh in the midst of such turmoil and pain.

When I returned to the United States nine months later as a hospital patient—I'd contracted a skin disease on my foot during the second acting tour of bases—I reapplied to college and continued my pre-enlistment studies, which foundered almost immediately. I'd been thrust back into a world of academia, of war-removed professors and giddy, just-out-of-high-school young women and men, none of whom seemed interested in the concerns of us few veterans. We ex-GIs clustered together, constantly exchanging overseas incidents and observations, keeping a real distance between us and our ingenuous fellow students. It was a lousy situation and our work suffered. Mine did, badly.

Months went by with no class improvement and no easing of my malaise about life, until a friend I'd been overseas with told me he was using his GI bill (tuition provided by the government for veterans) to attend an acting school. I didn't even know there was such a thing. I asked him how he got in, when he was going, and why. He said being an actor in Special Services was the only time in his life he felt free. I admitted that that was true for me, too. Feeling like I was risking a large hunk of my life, I also signed up for the acting school.

It was a decision I've never regretted.

Index of Exercises